31 DAYS OF CC

Without these people, I wouldn't have finished or done
this book
Andrew, Avril, Royce, Shanna, Stephanie

Contents

Introduction

I stumbled into contemplation, accidentally and spontaneously. These particular contemplations came about from October 2017 to August 2018. I wrote all of these days while being a licensed mental health counselor, and there is a lot of psychology and therapy in these words. These writings are as vulnerable as I can be up to this point in my life, and truly subjective. Inviting each other into our worlds is a worthwhile exercise in living. This has not been written or meant to be a diary. It's an attempt to communicate and write down my experiences of contemplation.

For the majority of writing, there was no plan set out before starting to write, except to just ride the wave. I did not have the motivation to be a commercial writer in doing this. I have never had a serious writing practice, and I have spent most of my creative energies focused on creating music. If these writings can have any benefit beyond my own experience of writing them, my greatest intention is that they can be models and sparks of igniting contemplation in the reader.

My individual consciousness became aware that my mind was uniquely my own by a single word, *what*. Immediately following this awakening by hearing the word *what* was the question, what came before me? I was riding home on a school bus in my elementary years, and in the midst of the chaos of white suburban road noise and children yelling at each other, my attention consumed this single question. What came before me?

There is no explanation for this; this was a surprise party welcoming me into myself, an unexpected gift left on my front door. I heard the knock and answered. To think now as an adult, that a child is capable of this experience! Recalling the story right now I am reminded that only with childlike openness can we begin a contemplative state.

The mystery *in and outside* of us awakens the inner observing self by using a question, and something paradoxical. A question represents an unknown. A truly good question provokes desire to enter into the unknown. Will we let ourselves right now be okay with our feelings of fear and anxiety the unknown creates? I have come to find that a truly worthwhile contemplative thought leads us with fear and confidence. In contemplation, we are able to hold fear and peace while looking at the unfamiliar, the nameless, the new and infinite within. These are all the places we have been running from for too long.

Describing how I fell into contemplation starts with these questions that entered into my young mind: what came before me, then from there, what came before them, then, what came before the earth, then, what came before the stars, what was before the darkness of space, and finally what was before all of this, what came before God? What is the void, whose idea was all of this, why did they put this burden of existence on me give me enough intelligence to even ask these questions?

I used this idea of God without really having an idea of God (I had not received any theological dogma up to that point in my life); I knew something had created me, my parents, so something must have created the universe. This is a simple rationale, I have no claim to know or understand the beginnings of everything, and I do not feel contemplation is supposed to give answers to that question. This is just the beginning of my contemplation.

My mind entered into a mantra of a cyclical question, what was before God? The question kept repeating itself faster and faster in my mind, and I had no answer. When the mind has no answer, something else inside has the chance to speak. I was probing and staring into the void, hearing and feeling my consciousness go to work with all the mental energy I had to find the answer.

The question and words quickly aroused in my heart a deep yearning, and all my being became enraptured in this question of unknowing, and into the pursuit of being *with* the unknowing—I was entering into a contemplative state of being. At first, there was a thrashing in the waves, trying to stay above water, and then there was a calm, and unification with the waves, moving and floating in the chaos.

This moment was so powerful for me and my *developmentally* young mind, that I disassociated, my actual material vision turned to pure white, I do not know if my eyes were opened or closed, and I felt as if I was floating above my body. I am confident that this was not just my childlike imagination. This was my actual lived experience. I felt as if I was a ghost floating three feet above the brown leather seats and heads of the chattering kids. I knew immediately that I loved this moment; it was a rush, I felt injected with some euphoric drug.

As my attention came to rest on this state of being, I quickly came back to the school bus and was back in my normal state. I tried to recreate the moment soon after, but was unsuccessful. I came close to recreating this moment in the weeks and months that followed, but none was quite as powerful as that first moment, and at each new attempt, the feeling and fantastical experience faded. That was my introduction and pursuit into contemplative practice, as a barely conscious child.

Contemplation is not about achieving a high or dissociative experience. Contemplation is about acknowledging all of ourselves, fears and hopes—and the space we inhabit between the unknown, and known of our external reality. Contemplation can come at any developmental age and at any moment, if we are willing to be still enough to hear with our true selves and allow our bodies to feel all of our emotions.

Contemplation is not religious or part of a religion, and in contemplation, we can hold and examine religious thoughts. I did not write this book with a motivation of proselytizing any religion. I would also like the reader to know that Christianity has greatly affected my understanding of contemplation and understanding of the unconditional and non-consumerist materialist realities in my life. Mindfulness practice and Buddhism have also influenced me tremendously as pathway into contemplation.

Meditation seems to lead to contemplative states, and both seem to come to similar conclusions. Meditation and mindfulness are a discipline of focus and attention, of inhabiting the void and detaching from suffering and desire. Contemplation begins with a thought and leads to internal and external actions of love, peace and hope. Contemplation is connection with self, nature and the other, and is not detaching from these realities, it is causing radical and full engagement with these realities, with stoicism and compassion. Contemplation is the wonder of the suddenness of thoughts and life changing ideas that have been there all along inside you waiting to come to the surface. Peace, Hope and love precede and proceed through it all.

Contemplative states have caused transcendence, deep intuitive peace, and acceptance to permeate my awareness. At times, I became aware of gentle euphoria. I have used psychedelics in the past and I do not know how to distinguish the difference between the two states of being, except there is no distinct come down during contemplation. I do not want to presume that this is a reality for everyone during contemplation, because feelings can be deceptive and pursuing those things is very fleeting. I think the feeling helps me know I am on the right track, maybe akin to a runner's high, a byproduct of doing something difficult that has positive benefits.

I feel the use of drugs at times can be a substitute for contemplative states. Drugs expand consciousness by creating new and novel experiences that cause us to experience others, the world and ourselves in a different way. We use drugs simply because the reality we are experiencing is not enough, we are searching for something more, whether that is a physical sensation, or just out of absolute boredom. We seem to be always seeking for something more within ourselves and outside of ourselves.

Contemplation too is expanding our consciousness and allowing us to see the other, the world and ourselves in a new and different way. I have come to see that the more I contemplate the less I really need things to alter my reality, the less I crave mind-altering substances. This too goes along with regular mindfulness practice, finding contentment with the moment is the ultimate intrinsic reward and real accomplishment.

In writing these 31 days of contemplation, I did it for myself and with a desire to put something into the world that would encourage and add psychological and existential depth to others. I simply started each day by calming my mind or doing mindfulness, until I had focus and attention on my mind and body. I would then allow whatever came up out of the void of consciousness (the silence and blackness in my mind) to arise, and use that as my starting point for the writing. On that school bus, what came up was what came before all of this. Sometimes these thoughts would occur to me randomly while looking out a window, or on the metro bus (there is obviously something for me about being on buses, the airport has the same effect on me), again when we are open we can stumble upon amazing things in any moment of our day.

I am able to recognize contemplative thoughts by being aware of, what I would call my *spirit,* or the part of me that is aware of awareness. My spirit is my core; the physical location is in my body and is right where my gut and my heart meet I would say, and from that place, there is a projection up into my head. The contemplative thoughts that arise from this void - create peace, longing, and curiosity are propelling me towards more authenticity, love, humility, peace and hope. Those attributes are how I know I am on the right path. There is an intuitive subjective knowing and realization in contemplation of, this is me, and this is the unknown calling me deeper into myself and engagement with the world, or perhaps another angle is to shed away that which is blinding me from my connection to everything else around me.

What I want others to gain in reading these days is a starting point into contemplative thought. By experiencing someone else's contemplation, hopefully the readers will be motivated into their own journey of contemplation. Contemplation has always been the chord that has pulled me out of dark wells, and given me hope in times of despair. Contemplation has never failed me once and has always been worth the time. Contemplation has taught me that I am worth taking the time to see my own value and the value of all that is around me.

Many of these sentences are better read slowly; the sentences repeated over again two or three times while reading. I wrote these words slowly and typically breathed the sentences in and out. I was not in a frantic or manic state. Think of breathing in a calm and deliberate pace, the thoughts came at that speed. Sometimes I did however, want to push and not be patient, which did not help.

These readings are an exercise in contemplation, of entering into something inside the self, an opening up of our senses. I want these words to heighten someone's sense of their internal and external reality, which can feel like an altered state of old looking new. I hope that anyone who reads this finds their ever-present self-worth, the reality of love, the forever incoming of hope and the knowledge of discovering a foundation of peace—and will engage with those four things, with themselves and with the other. You can read this book one day at a time, or not. Again, I wrote these words slowly, I suggest reading them slowly. Contemplation is a way to grow in spiritual awareness, a way to be your own guru and enlivened by the mystery of being a being.

Mindfulness Exercise

As I mentioned in the introduction, most of these contemplations were done after mindfulness practice, and typically were written in one sitting. I also, while writing, listened to music that connected me to this contemplative part of myself, typically I was listening to the duo called, Stars of the Lid, either the album, *And Their Refinement of the Decline* or *The Tired Sounds of Stars of the Lid.* I share those albums, because the emotion that music evokes matches my contemplative state. I do not think music has to have anything to do with contemplation, music just personally works for me, I am a musician, and it was my first language.

To practice mindfulness I like to set aside 20 minutes of uninterrupted time, I think a minimum of 5 minutes is needed. We are supposed to hold our attention on one thing at a time; typically, the breath is the place to start. When our minds get distracted being pulled from this place of attention, all we can do is gently bring our minds back to the object of attention. Breathing in and out, while focusing on the entirety of the breath, the physical sensation of the breath entering and leaving, even the moments of nothingness after a total exhalation and inhalation.

We can also do a slow body scan. We put all our attention starting at the tips of our toes, feeling the temperature of our feet, the texture of our socks, anything that is noticeable and slowly working our way through our whole bodies. I love doing this. If there is pain and tension in a specific part, that is fine, perhaps just breath in the tension and then exhale that tension, perhaps try not to breathe that tension back in.

I will typically count my breaths to 100, one inhalation and one exhalation equals one breath. After that, I will do a full body scan. After scanning all the main parts of my body, I will allow thoughts to come in and out of my consciousness just listening and observing the narrator in my head. During this, it is important to note that thoughts are not you, the voice in your head is not fully you, awareness is you, we *are aware of the thoughts, and we are not our thoughts.* Awareness does not change, thoughts feelings, external experiences change. We are the same awareness at 5 years old and 95 years old.

Next, I will typically observe whatever images come into my mind, however random or stimulating they might be, I am just a mere observer of all these things. No image is good or bad. Next, I bring my attention to my emotions, and observe them, whatever that emotion might be, I simply observe, while knowing I am not my emotion, I have emotions that are a part of me.

Finally, I try to see if I can just be aware of being aware. This part for me is what I interpret to be a state of meditation. This awareness of only awareness, this state of consciousness that has been observing and been the same since childhood, and will take us all the way to our death, if we are coherent at that time of when we pass into the ultimate unknown. This observer does not change, although our bodies and the external world affect it. This observer is not a singular thought, emotion, or a body...there is mystery here.

In this state of simple awareness of awareness, is typically when the contemplative thought will come. Arising from that place between where my physical heart and gut join in my body. Sometimes the thought could be about the dishes that need to be washed, or remembering a dream I had. If it comes to me from this place, I need to listen and follow. Most of the time this voice, feels very old and familiar, almost like déjà vu. From there I just allow the whole process to unfold, floating with the waves of feelings and thoughts up and down. I know I am on the right waves if at the end I am lead to a knowledge and experience of peace, hope or love.

We do not have to try to act spiritual or be anything else in contemplation, because contemplation is a natural state, when we are not resisting ourselves. In this state, we are our own gurus.

Eventually in life, we make a decision to believe something about all of this (existence). Whether we believe what someone is teaching us, or we seek it out ourselves, at some point we make a decision. I think getting clarity on what is causing us to decide on a belief of nihilism, agnosticism, atheism, or full on following religious doctrine, is a foundation of being. Contemplation is always worth our time no matter what belief system we adhere to.

Spend this time with yourself, fully knowing and acknowledging all of your conscious experience. Everything can be taught to a certain point, in the end we have to experience ourselves doing and being contemplative to really learn. The simplest way for me to understand the beginning of contemplation is being open. Now let us be open.

Day 1

I want to find peace, hope and love unconditionally residing inside of me. There is also a constant void that coincides and lives with those desires, and is equally a part of me. The void is the space in between who I am, the person I am consciously aware of, and possibility. How will I react to the Void Unknown? I keep returning to the void repeatedly, and in that space, there is only silence and darkness. The void exists, and is the mystery that I love to seek and what I am terrified of. The unknown in and outside of me causes me terror in the middle of the night. The void, contemplation and me create the ultimate *worthwhile* mystery of which I must participate. The mystery, the void and I are tied together inexplicably, what an experience to be alive!

The search internal, the journey into consciousness, reveals layers of mystery, based in a void. They say there is a God shaped hole in the heart of man, there is a part of us that craves wonder, mystery and finding meaning in suffering. In that hole a void is revealed, something that once was there or perhaps was never there—a standalone void sewn into the fabric of consciousness, or the imprint of something *wholly other*. When I return to the internal search inside my mind and body, I feel like I am dancing around the void, with a partner that might have been or never was there. I assume it is either a programmed evolutionary dance, or maybe the dance with some wholly other, a totally unknowable partner.

When I was 16 years old I believed I heard a voice come out of the void inside my head, it was during a moment of prayer and seeking, I simply heard my full name being spoken, Joshua...Joshua. I responded with, is that you God, where are you. The voice in my head said, I've been here the whole time. It was in that moment that I realized that there was a part of my consciousness that had been speaking to me since childhood, and in that moment I made a connection to this voice being God, God is within me—the existence of a God consciousness.

There is something greater within my consciousness to be sought after and is worth the seeking. With contemplation there is something tangible to work with. Today this voice has become so apart of me; it does not seem foreign enough, to be some external creator speaking to me in my *spirit*. I would not say that particular feeling was a contemplative experience; I simply learned that there are voices inside that pull us towards deeper meaning. So what am I doing in contemplation except, as always, returning to the mystery—I must always be returning.

The feeling and call to contemplation within a dream:

I woke up once in a dried out lakebed, about 15 miles round, surrounded by pale purple blue mountains. The ground was cracked and the air was warm enough to not notice either a warmth or coolness. The sun was about to rise in the next 15 minutes and as I looked around at the mountains, I had found that in this place the impossible was real, since all possibilities existed in infinite directions here.

The mountains said to me, be still. I felt I could stay in this place for an eternity; I wanted to stay, because this is the truest peace I had felt yet. I did not have any thought about asking how I had woken up here; a question would have broken the spell. As I adjusted to this new reality, of solitude and connection, a young woman, or a girl who had just become grown was approaching me from the right.

She was walking at a pace that was hurried, yet put me at ease all at the same time. She wore white, and the light was starting to change the colors all around her. She came to me, we were at peace with each other, although complete strangers. She acknowledged me without having to look at me and I felt safe. She bent down right next to me and started to write in the dried out clay of the cracked lakebed.

I intuitively knew she came here for this reason, to write a message in the lakebed. She might have been doing it for 1000 years. I knew that she had not come there for me, but she was not disturbed to see my intrusion. She did not welcome me nor refuse me. I felt I must read what she wrote; this message must be an answer, or *the* answer. I could not decipher the writing; it was like a language I use to know, and had long forgotten.

When she was done, she turned to me and said, "We must leave this place, the water is returning soon." How can I leave this place, I had just gotten here, this was the place I have been wanting to be found in, as long as I have known I have wanted something. However, there was some sense of danger, and I was a foreigner in this land, and she obviously the local. I obeyed and followed her out of the lakebed into the surrounding hills. I still have yet to return to that place, in the same way or form.

She led me for some time through hills, until we finally came to the place of exiting. It was morning now, everything seemed to be reflecting light, or maybe everything was giving off its own type of light. She had led me to a salt-water bay, with a few docks. There were people around, but no one stood out to me.

As I scanned my environment, in the distance there was a woman standing by a boat. She was placing her hand along the wooden hull, and caressing it, as if the boat was alive and some sort of giant gentle beast. My heart was filled with longing to go to be with this person, to leave on this boat into something unknown with her. Contemplation was calling.

I realize now how strange it is that I had quickly forgotten the lakebed and all it's desolation, and the complete rapture of my being, as I stood and waited for her to look at me. Peace and possibility led me to this contemplation invitation; I could not just go and leave everything behind. I wanted this moment to last and go on forever, but it did not and could not. I woke up again, always returning.

Do I want to find God, within me or outside of me? Do I want God to be a creator a ruler or a moral judge? Do I want God to be preached to me or taught to me by someone, or a complete subjective internal experience? Is God just a feeling or the idea of hope, peace and unconditional love? Do I need God to become my true self, and a loving human being? Is recognizing my lack the first step in becoming something more than I am, and is God who I turn to, to transform me. Is God just a feeling or a belief to push the void away, an evolutionary fail-safe against madness?

Is the unconditional God? Is the unconditional a trace of a left behind snakeskin, of something that is real and living near or far? Can I be pleased with just a trace, is only knowing the trace enough? Is questioning an exercise that strengthens me? Is death my greatest teacher and guide?

If ruling my consciousness is the goal of all this, then I must not limit my influence from the outside world, because then I limit possibility—and the outside world is what I cannot ever totally control. The more variables and chaos the more chances for something new to emerge. I am always craving this new possibility. Ruling consciousness is a goal, but not an end.

Consciousness is a tricky thing, fragile like a bubble travelling through the air. Therefore, we try to rule our consciousness and ground it in something. I can ground it in moral spiritual teachings, in philosophy, in partying and in faith commitments. The one thing I do know is that my consciousness wants to be united with something else, beside itself. My consciousness wants to be totally revealed to me, to itself, and to the other—and wholly other, the void, the unknown. I want to remove whatever blocks and limits my awareness of myself and of the other, fully engaged and open to all possibilities, like in that dried out lakebed.

Day 2

Another dream, contemplation has to expand the distance between consciousness and the subconscious, the full spectrum of awareness, sometimes I must start with that other worldly subconscious dream and listen to that message

As I looked down over the railing, I saw two of my trusted friends standing in my living room, which had become a great cathedral expanse. I did not know how to get down to them, and they looked up at me, as if they had sent me off, knowing that perhaps danger lay ahead of me—but signaling with their expressions that they would stay down there all the same. This was a still comfort that gave me enough purpose to keep exploring my childhood home.

I remembered this kitchen, brown wooden cabinets with a yellowish floor. I was bigger now, so everything seemed so much smaller. I went back out to look over the railing, down into the living room and they were thankfully still there.

As I turned back towards the kitchen, I noticed a ladder leading up to a dimly lit loft. I looked back towards my friends, and they gave me the same expression of fear mixed with hope—the look we give to someone before they are about to have a lifesaving surgery.

I decided with curiosity to see what was in this new addition to my old home. I climbed the ladder and stood to my feet. There were tables with leftover party plates and hats, and a soda fountain was at the back that you could tell was used to make milkshakes. It seemed like a scene out of the 1950's, but felt like the 1980's.

The only light was coming from a single wall fixture at the back of the wall. I was now starting to see that these were the remnants of a child's birthday party, a scene of innocence all of a sudden turned into the deepest feeling of despair. There was something hauntingly sad about seeing these artifacts of a party that might have ended 2 hours to 22 years ago, I could not tell, but I could feel the ghosts of joy that remained in that room.

The dim light called me in closer, and as I answered this call by walking closer to the leftovers of the party, my heart struck me down with terror, as if crossing a forbidden boundary. I collapsed to the floor no longer being able to stand, due to the overwhelming emotion emanating from within my chest, and radiating out through every fiber of my physical being. I laid there face first, glued to the ground weeping, a complete catharsis of emotion. I wanted and did not want to look back to that lonely light at the back of the room.

All of a sudden right before I was going to be lost forever to despair, a familiar voice spoke to me and said, you have to face this and feel this pain. It was my own voice, of contemplation, in my head; I knew it spoke the *truth*. I felt comforted by this correction and knew it was true; this was an experience of total joy and total innocence lost, in the same moment.

This moment felt more right to me than any other moment I have had. The realization of this moment came with great fear and comfort. The fear of knowing that both ultimate joy and sorrow are married together—the two sides of the same coin. I never was able to make it to the back of that room, back to where the light was calling to me, to where perhaps clarity would have been given. I knew that I had found the innocence and loss of innocence that was inside some trauma of me.

Something is lost inside of me...something is lost inside of me...lost inside of...lost inside...lost inside of me. Something is hidden inside of me. I am hidden inside of me. There is something lost inside of me, and how can I find it. I am lost inside of me, and how can I find myself. If it is inside of me, than it is a part of me, it is just lost. If I am inside of me than I am a part of me, I am just lost. How can I find this lost part of me?

Stop looking for answers and start feeling it all. Start feeling all of myself. Stop living in the darkness and start living in the light, stop living in the light and start living in the darkness. Stop trying to live life all alone, and start being brave in facing your isolation. Start acknowledging all of your past trauma and innocence, and acknowledging that everything has changed. Listen to your body and your thoughts. Be willing to accept your loss and hold on to the sweetness of your memories. Be nostalgic while expecting the impossible unknown good to come. Stop rating yourself and the day, and be willing to accept disappointment.

Trauma conceals apart of ourselves to ourselves. Trauma traps inside whatever the trauma took away; trauma traps the healing behind a closed door. I must go where I have not been in a long time inside myself, and know the darkness and the light inside. I must accept myself—trust that joy is still there, scared and waiting to reveal myself to myself. There will be no more children's parties, and the spirit of the child remains inside.

Lest I become like a child and not be ashamed of my desire for innocence, I will not know peace. Welcome back and find your innocence, and your peace and wonder at living. Tremble with the sorrow and joy, as I literally shake myself free from the loss, and find the innocent child within.

These things reside in the contemplative mind: our questions, the void, peace, hope, love, transcendence and our malaise—and all at times lead to a stuck feeling of unknowing. Are we getting use to this unknowing? When we allow ourselves to become supremely focused on this state of unknowing, something other emerges within the self. No matter how atheistic I can be or how much of a believer I can be, there is a question in me. A question shows evidence of a speaker and a seeker. True and open seeking creates altered states, and will I dare to listen to the question calling out to me.

How far am I willing to go into the question, the unknowing, can I strip myself totally naked of everything that makes me feel secure. To let go of superego societal and religious beliefs, as well as my id driven desires for physical and material needs and pleasures. This is what and where I will be within myself when I enter contemplation.

Into the question I will go, and what is my question today, what am I seeking today? Is it more than, what will I eat for lunch and how will I entertain myself tonight until I am tired enough to fall asleep. What is the question that arouses my deepest fears, that is it, that is the one I must go into boldly and in complete humility?

I must face that question completely with no fear of the consequences, of knowing or not knowing. The questions of: am I utterly alone here, will I ever know the love my intuition knows exists and that I resist and cannot find, can my life have meaning beyond my limitations, what is making this universe keep going, where did my innocence go, why don't I fully trust anyone, how did I decide hating myself was the right idea, why do I feel unlovable, what is this fear that fills my stomach, why don't I believe in God, why do I believe in God, what was I like as a child, what is unconditional love, how can I experience this moment fully without judging?

Now I sit with these questions and allow the full experience to happen. The full cognitive experience of complete optimistic and pessimistic thought, and the full emotional experience of dread and peace, both of these moments must happen, and coalesce into contemplation.

The moment I close off to one of these experiences, I miss the chance to experience the other, the high and the low. As I allow both experiences to happen they balance and mix and create a new color, maybe a color I have never seen before. Something new emerges, if it is truly new, then this is evidence of hope, and with hope, love is sure to follow—with love comes the possibility to enjoy the self and enjoy the other. Love allows for the chance of peace, and if I have peace, than I have entered into contemplation, through dread and hope.

Peace is what I need, peace with myself, with the other, with nature and with the unknowing or the void. Peace that stems from a question within the self and is answered within the self in humility and courage. Question is a word, a sound uttered through vocal chords, but what the question really means to me; is to acknowledge the existential roots the word sprung from, to see that in the question is spiritual life.

Help me help myself, embrace the void, then help the other, the other who helps me, face and answer the unknowing question that awoke me, to me, a unique individual. To find the spirit within, hearing my individual unique one of kind subjective self, my spirit, calling to the unknowing within me.

What question is arising inside of you right now in this moment, now spend a moment with yourself, and allow this question to be, without fear

Open your eyes meet and greet the day. Hello light, hello decisions-with-consequences, hello bodily needs and waking consciousness. How will I greet you today, what will my heart harbor towards you—reticence and drudgery or openness and wonder, either way both ways of being are still possible regardless of the conditions. A condition of plenty or scarcity, my heart decides how to greet the new day.

We have had to greet each other every day since the day I was born. I use to wonder if maybe I would wake up from a long dream someday, and be a baby all over again—life just one long continuous dream inside a dream. The first moment of contact with the day, might be the most important. As if the first moment of each day was a first impression, and would color how the next 16 hours will be experienced. Awakening from a dream, in the morning light or in darkness, how will I greet this day?

Will I curse you for waking me up, or feel nothing at all. Will I run away back underneath the covers, like a slap in the face? How will I decide to come out of my subconscious activities of sleep, and step into the reality of being back in my body, laying on a bed, on a small planet in the Milky Way, which is stuck in orbit around a star in an infinite universe? Those two realities compete for my soul every morning, to return to sleep or to step into the infinite possibility of all of *this*, which is what greets me each new day, how will I respond back?

To return to sleep is to stonewall and abuse the inevitable, my chance to engage in life. I could sleep and refuse to rise until my body shuts down from lack of nutrients and then to the finality of death. To shy away from the day and to prefer the total isolation of my dream world is surely death both physical and mental. To prefer sleep is mental quicksand sucking me further into helplessness and the belief that I have no control. Oh, how I love sleep I tell myself, sleep, sleep, sleep, and maybe you will not have to do any of this. Yet I still rise.

It is not a matter of sleeping or not sleeping, it is a matter of rising. How will I rise, under what power will I fling my legs over the side of my bed, flex my stomach and neck and bring myself standing to an upright position. Will I live from fear that causes my body to respond to its command, fear of financial ruin, or is there a greater motivator? Fear has been my greatest motivator; fear *the ultimate* mover and shaker of humankind. Fear, what have I to do with you today.

How will I greet this day, under what forced conditions will I have to decide to transcend fear today? I need a new means and greeting, one that causes me to rise in assurance and unknowing expectation. One that says I am me and I am the only me, and I am ready to be me in this far off corner of the universe. One that takes the indifference and molds me into something abstract, and can allude and intimidate past demons of despair, malaise and anxiety.

I will be shy when I greet the day, and totally open all at the same time. I need a sense of the total newness of the day, like the feeling before the first date with someone I have had a crush on. I will not run back inside my mind, dodging the confrontation with the unknown. The confrontation of interacting with a world I cannot fully control and fully know. The confrontation of being thrown into a world full of totally other: the totally otherness of nature, will it rain or will it quake, the totally otherness of my fellow human, will I be praised or will I be rejected, and the totally otherness of the universe, will the aliens finally invade or will we continue in our complete isolation.

Yes, I will rise, greet the day, and keep all of what I just spoke in my heart dearly. I will believe in the infinite possibilities of whatever.

*Contemplation equals a beginning of authenticity with the
very real and different parts of the self.*

Where can I run to escape you, in my mind I see
myself running out the back door, barefooted onto the wet
grass? I run and get as far as the driveway and cannot
imagine going any further, to go further would be to flirt
with madness. I cannot ever escape you, you keep me
captive, and why do you want to keep me so close all the
time. I do not ever recall making a decision to be here, to
be here with you every day. A decision to even be at all. I
am being held here against my will. Yet I know that if I
were to escape, I would disappear into unconsciousness,
disintegrate into nothingness and meaninglessness—a
nihilism that has finally come true.

Escape has never been an option, like being stuck
in a capsule floating in outer space, if I were to leave this
lifeboat and you; I would be instantly consumed by the
blackness and vacuum of total darkness.

Where are we going on this journey and how did
you bring me here, why are you bringing me along? How
many times will I have to ask you, where did you find me,
what tree was I plucked from? When will you start to see
how scared I am, I have been concealing my insanity from
you, if you will just answer me these simple questions, I
might feel welcomed and want to stay.

With a simple pause and flick of the mental wrist, I
see that we are like elastic, attached and stuck together.
That pulling away from you is pulling away from me. You
are not keeping me here; I am keeping me here. You are a
part of me; I am you through and through. To run away,
is to run away from me. To run away, is just running
away from my mind. I cannot get any further away from
you, without losing my self and mind.

The more I question you the emptier I feel. The more I do not want to be me and the more I do not want to be in this place with you, the more I become *the* embodiment of anxiety. My body starts to disintegrate inside as I try to hide and run from me. Hatred grows as I reject myself. It grows to a fever pitch as the terror sets in, in the rejection of myself. I become an impenetrable prison of doubts and blindness.

All wars have had their beginning first within the internal battle of self-hatred in the hearts of human beings. Before a rock was ever thrown, a rock was lodged within the self. The war between the, am I love or am I nothingness.

This war within the self, of the battling of the unknown within, can be the start of all healing. I am I and I am a self. Come back inside and get to know all of yourself, step away from the door and get to know you. Stop wanting to not to be a self, so you do not have to be accountable for acknowledging you exist. You can be scared, that is allowed, and there is an anchor to be found inside you.

Even if I never asked to be here awake in consciousness, there is still an anchor to be found inside myself. Look and feel inside. This anchor tugs gently at my heart and wraps around my guts firmly tying it to the depths below. I look down and see it going into infinity-- that is when I know I am truly safe and tied to something real. Anchored to infinity and an unknowable depth.

I call below, why did you bring me here, to the depths inside, as Victor Frankl says, if there is no answer, now I know I am speaking to the right place within me, to the infinite place. The blank response signals that there is no bottom, nothing for the sound to reflect back to me, an infinite space inside myself. This lack of response, silent treatment, is not a rejection; it is an invitation luring me in, to experience myself alone.

Let this anchor drift and hold me firm in place, firm in the infinity inside myself. I can only be a whole self, be comfortable in myself, by acknowledging this infinity inside me. To not run from myself, and greet the intangible inside, is to become rooted and accepting of the unknown, and how it is embracing me. To embrace myself back, is when a deep peace will take hold of me. To know peace is to know who I really am.

Be inside myself; be alone, fully inside my mind and body. Feel the depth of your unique existence knowing that it has been given as an unconditional gift of love. To know all this and still have peace, is to allow love to grow. Ignore the lies of accusation that I am a mistake. Life is never a mistake when it is seen through the lens of love.

There is no fear in love. If I fear myself and want to run from me, love is still waiting to be found. Even in doubt, right now in this moment, with a hand over my heart I say, may I know love, may I know peace, and may I be found. Come and find me and I will go with you, with the love that created me, whether unknown or known love, I wait for this love.

My self was given to me unconditionally. I will not run away from me any longer, I will remain in the unknown and infinity within. I am learning how to be alone with all of me. I know I am not alone when I am fully with all of me.

Nothing compares to right now, to this moment, to this very instant, I must ask myself what is wrong with now. There might be nothing I like about the conditions of right now, yet I must still know that nothing is wrong with right now. There is nothing inherently wrong with being fully engaged with the present, since there is no other fantasy now to be accessed; and the only alternative is drifting off into an awake state of dreaming, which has been my preferred alternative for too many years.

To not be fully engaged in this now, is to be in a dream world. To live in a dream is a phantasmagoric nightmare, where we are puppet ghosts with no strings attached. We will feel hollow and empty in this state, there is nothing solid inside and we become totally helpless to the external pressures and changes. The only moment that exists is now; the only sure reality that can be accurately perceived is right now. The only true peace I can have is right now. If I am to feel fear, it is right now, to be anywhere else in my mind except here in my body and in this space, is to be asleep. To not be fully immersed in right now, is to be a ghost in the land of the living. When I ruminate in thoughts of the past or figuring out the future, I am not living, I am two-dimensional, I am half-awake.

Trauma, the impossible bad, it robs us of our ability to be right now. To disassociate in the middle of trauma, is a gift that is to be used before the moment of death, but to continue on in trauma after it has passed, is to continue on in the rejection of right now. To not live in the moment of now, is to have not realized that the nightmare is over, it has already past, you are awake, and new possibilities are waiting to be sought and accepted. To not be able to accept right now is to be truly alone in an ongoing temporary moment of trauma in a past that no longer exists. To constantly be living the narrative of the wrongness of now is my trauma narrative of the past, a ghost existing and eclipsing the real moment of now.

I want to know if I am truly awake, anything that would lead me to feel the contrary, would signal that I am rejecting right now, rejecting this very moment to come into contemplation. To not accept and reject the now is to come out of reality and into speculation. To say, "what is truth, it doesn't exist?" is to not be experiencing everything that is happening right now internally and externally. Truth is right now. To reject the material world or the inner spiritual world is to go on living in some dream, where you are not the author or participant of anything. Whether I am dreaming because I am disconnected to inner me, or rejecting the outer world, I need to come and accept the now of both realities, and merge the internal and external.

I have an ancient body and a new mind. My brain is millennia older than I am. My mind is fresh, new, and malleable every day, susceptible to all that is around me and inside of me. I have ancient desires to run, fight and reproduce without consequence—and my mind wants to travel from star to star.

I have an ancient body and a modern mind. My mind must ride the waves of this ancient body, what it feels and what it is trying to teach me. My body is me, and to reject any part of me is to be partially asleep. Just as a part of my body will fall asleep and become numb and unmovable when it is forgotten about and not in use, it is the same to not accept all of now—I become numb and unmovable as parts of me fall asleep.

My mind rejects the carried history of this body, with all its emotions and feelings; it says something is wrong with now. It wants to be free of this material weight, not live in the now of gravity and slow cellular decay. My body does not want to go where my spiritual mind is leading me, it cannot fit into that space—its material being cannot breathe and survive where my contemplation is leading. My body does not want to live in the now of the endless possibilities within the mind and subjective inner experience.

Yet my mind and body must be at peace with each other if they are both to be real and not asleep, they must be one in agreement of engaging right now and loving the other.

Being in the now with you and finding me

Open up your eyes and you will find a black hole, a void, in the middle of a supernova of light. Our eyes take everything in, and let nothing out. The eyes are the window to the soul, yet what do I see when I look at you. I see a void in the center; I see the reflection of my own void in you. Will I live awake in this moment of now, or will I live with my eyes closed, not seeing you and in turn not seeing me. Will I keep refusing to truly look at you, because I refuse to look at me?

The level of fear I feel when I look at you, is the level of fear I feel towards me. Will I look honestly into your eyes and get sucked up in the void? If I know, nothing is wrong with now, than the answer is yes. I will look into your eyes, and - stare peacefully into a void of the other. Maybe if I look long enough I will start to see me in you, and the true impossibility of breaking my isolation will show that we are not alone, as I once believed. *Maybe I can only accept me, by accepting the void I see in you.*

I will look at you and know nothing is wrong with the now of you, the existence of you—so I can accept the existence of me. There is a connection between the rejections of now, when I am rejecting the other.

To not reject the now, and to know that there is nothing wrong with now, will be a step towards knowing the other, truly looking into their eyes and the pupil that lets out no light. In this acceptance of the other, comes an acceptance of the self. To avoid the void in the middle of the other's eye is to avoid looking at your own reflection. Even if I cannot see, I still can feel the presence of the other, the weight of their body that changes the material fabric around me. There is nothing wrong with right now, right now is how I must be.

Whether my body is warm or cold, or my mind is disorganized or centered, I must wake up and be living right now. And hear myself ask, what is wrong with now, and my gentle response back only knows silence, there is, or there is not anything wrong.

I do not want to be unsure of reality any longer. I do not want to be a ghost wandering an island in the middle of the ocean in the dark, trying to find a way out. To get off this island, I must realize first if I am rejecting this moment in anyway. When I stop rejecting the now, then I will see a bridge. This bridge will lead me across dark waters to a station, where trains will be departing all the time. It does not matter which train I choose, I must just decide to get on. As I board the train I look one last time to see where I am going, and I see it says, *the train to everywhere.* I am on the train to everywhere, to every possible destination, to every possible moment of being alive—to every possibility of right now. We start to pull out, and we come into the light of a new consciousness. My mind and the core of who I am know that everything is all right.

In every depression let there be light, or in every depression, there is light. Depression is the loss of motivation, the loss of the motivator within the self. What once was there, motivating pulling you forward has now collapsed and formed a concave lens in the chest—the chest turns inward forming a funnel sucking everything in, the weight of existence too heavy to bear. Where has the motivator within gone, the giver and feeder of life?

Searching for this light within depression a teacher emerges, named death. Of course death would be found here, as it is the ultimate sense of something gone and lost, a major characteristic of depression is the intuition that something is missing. Death finds me and becomes the ultimate teacher of avoiding depression, because when facing true death that is when we see how much we want to live.

Suicide is a sickness, a wrong connection to depression and death. Suicide as sickness must be seen as a temporary disorder and needing the appropriate treatment. Suicide when acted on in impulse is nothing more than a tragedy of a temporary state of despair, and a misrelating to the self. Death's greatest mission is to bring life, not end it. If I will engage with death, I can begin to engage with life. In depression there is a teacher named death, but not the death that ends your life. It is where death is trying to show you how to truly live, by living from and acknowledging the internal self.

Depression is a feeling of loss, the loss of a part of me, a part of my life that has gone and been traded for some other self that is not truly all of me. The feelings of depression (loss, death, sadness, etc.), or the desire for death, can simply be a miss-relation to the self within. Depression is a sinking feeling a void within the chest, calling me back within. Will I listen to this call and follow this feeling inside myself, realizing that what is dying inside wants to come to life, if I will only turn to myself.

A desire for death, feelings of depression and the loss of the motivator, is not related to ending physical existence, but has everything to do with a desire for the death of a false self. Every depression can be unique, there can be many forms of depression, but I am most interested in recognizing the depression that is calling me and leading me inside towards a vibrant inner life. I want to know the depression that is reminding me that something is dying inside, something is needing nurturing, focus and attending to. If I am to live, I cannot ignore this feeling any longer.

A Concave lens of depression within the chest does not produce a real image of a person. When people are not looking at themselves within the focal point of this lens in the chest (feeling, viewing and valuing themselves from a heartfelt perspective), the identity of the self is not based in reality, and the image is skewed and seen as something less desired. Depression is that feeling of something not feeling right inside our minds and bodies, we feel off, as if we are not right, we do not desire ourselves.

To get back into focus we must realize there are *two* lives to be lived, the *inner life* and *outer life*. Both lives must be seen, lived, and brought into focus for our true identity to emerge. The inner life must be valued and prized as much as the actor we play day to day in our bidding for praise and attention in the outer life. The inner life will wither and die when rejected, and we can become depressed.

The image we see when not living from the internal self-causes these inner images and feelings of depression, emptiness and a loss of hope. When moving away from the inner life, the further we move, the more distorted the image of our true identity will become-- and the greater the distortion, the greater the depression. Many psychologists know that depression is a bottling up of negative emotion, once the emotions are named and attended to the depression can start to lift—once we turn inside and look within.

My malaise is a reminder that my spirit remains; my malaise is a symptom, a fever of the inner self. My dissatisfaction and boredom are a testament of needing more motivation to live in life, than just passing through and focusing on my outer life, what and who I have or do not have. The feeling of loss of motivation is simply an invitation to find more motivation than to just live in the temporal and material world—an invitation to find hope and actual meaning.

Many times feelings of depression and defeat are the inner self's call to find more to live for than popularity, an alcohol induced buzz, or a life only energized and lived with pride when we have finally attained freedom of leisure, or not having to work as hard as everyone else. We trade one life for another, we over value the outer life, not recognizing that we are more than material vessels of consumerist desire to be advertised to—and shamed by our lack of youth or beauty.

The inner life does not desire death, and we will feel like we are grieving when we fail to acknowledge the beauty of the inner self. The feelings of this type of depression are a guiding light to find more in life than we thought possible.

Deep inside underneath the veil of my flesh I have known

That none of this has ever quite felt right

To have to earn everything we have underneath the sun

To have to earn the love that we burn,

To earn everything we have underneath our sun

Last's night's dream Edy was holding me and we were just trying to let ourselves be, happy

Don't stop holding me

You've been selling this dream for so well, for so long, to the acceptable addiction

To try and avoid the void

Now let withdrawal come soon, selling it all

If I could sell it all, I would really only need to sell my high-inflated value I place on all of this that lies outside of me. I would not actually have to sell one physical possession. I would only have to sell off the frantic attention and emotional energy I place on the outer known self and move my attention inward—to find the value of the inner self, because from within is the only place that peace and unconditional love can truly emerge.

Love can find us from outside of ourselves, but the unconditional love we find in ourselves creates unending ability and motivation to live. Peace can barely be found in an overvalued and large bank account, but peace found and nurtured within, is the only unconditional strength without limitations we will ever find.

Depression feels like death, that something is missing or that something has gone and seems like it will never come back. Depression when seen through contemplation is an invitation to find life and let other things become lost and go missing for a moment. Depression is a hunger to find motivation to live for something more than just the outer life. When having my inner life come more into focus, I see myself for who I am and see that I can live for more than just all of this external, there are riches to be found within, peace and love to be found within.

When depression is rooted in unbalanced brain chemistry, sometimes the first step to accessing the inward self is through medical intervention.

Day 8

May I be always proclaiming, I am not above a dish...I am not above a dish! My position is neither above nor below the task of washing a dish. A dish is neither above me nor below me, there is only the task of knowing what it means to clean a dish. A dirty dish, a sink full of dirty dishes awaits me motionless, waiting for something to happen.

Once they were clean, yet now they are dirty, waiting to be washed, to be usable again, and again and again. To be made dirty again, and again. To continue to be made dirty and clean without having a why, answer or a question, a repetition with no drummer and a command with no commander. I am to always be returning.

I stare at them, and they do not stare back at me, this is becoming a cosmic joke of epic proportions, utter ridiculousness, to even have a consciousness in the universe that can generate this thought; to even have a writer, compose these very words. I am not above a dish, and the truth is that everything in me wants to try to convince me that *I am above a dish*. How can this thought, I am not above a dish, caress and transform me, as I approach these dishes?

Why should I be tasked with such a meaningless procedure, to scrub clean my food waste, and even more distasteful than that, to have to scrub clean the food waste of another, some chaos I did not even create? I even have to wash another's dish! Will I allow something deep emerge from something so meaningless. To lower-myself to this position having to be equal, and servant to the dish and servant to the other. What is the presence in me that despises the dishwasher?

This dish cares nothing for me; it has no mind, which means it cares nothing for itself, for it has no self. Still I care so much about what it is I inevitably must do. And here I will be washing the dish, treating it as valuable, giving it care, so as not to break it, and restoring it to a state of newness. Treating the dish even better than I have treated myself today. For I see the dish and I see it needs help and attention, and I do something about it quickly. I am starting to fear now that not only am I not above a dish; I am in fact a servant of the dish. I am a servant to the task of finding purpose in washing a dish.

In deciding to wash a dish, I am washing the meaninglessness out of this dish. In removing the unnecessary waste from the dish, I am aligning myself with the unwanted. I am saying I am not above the unwanted; I am not above the meaninglessness of washing a dish. I am doing something meaningful. I am washing myself of the belief that there is emptiness in me doing something appearing so meaningless. I will too now wash myself of thinking that this is boring, as if boring was even something factual. Boredom is not real.

The only thing that is really happening is that I think I am above a situation that is placed before me—that I cannot find joy in washing a dish. That is real. When will I be willing to go to a place in my mind and body, where I am not above a dish? Yet I know that I am not above the dish, nor is the dish above me, I am still just searching inside for someone.

And who is this someone, this someone has to be me, the dishwasher waiting to be found inside of me. The great and heroic dishwasher that is tired of being shamed, that wants to live and grow, and show the great power and strength in simply washing a dish. In being, willing to do what is unwanted. I will wash the dish, and let the dishwasher inside of me, wash me of all my false arrogance of ever thinking I am above a dish.

48

Why will the meek inherit the earth, it is because they are the only ones worthy of this earth. They are the only ones willing to truly and blamelessly wash a dish, and find the glory in the dish. They are the true ones that know there is no dish. There is only simple labor, to let simplicity even grow into a labor of love, of laboring for no great gain, esteem or prize. To take importance in doing what others say is meaningless, by never questioning or judging if I am worth being alive by doing simplicity. The resolution is in the willingness to labor without judging the value of what it is I am doing.

The meek will inherit the earth for they are the only ones capable of causing the ones in power to stumble. The arrogant will stumble by their reaction to the sudden bubbling up of compassion that has been dormant in their soul, as they refuse to close and turn their backs on the meek. The meek can cause all this to happen, by their ability to have grace in washing the dish in love—and that power found in peace will rise inside of me as I receive that I am not above a dish.

So then, there is even glory in the dish. In the dish there is a glory and freedom—a freedom in finding your meekness. Meekness is strength, it is love, and it empowers you to know you are not above a dish, because there is no dish. There is only the willingness to just be in total acceptance of the appearance of meaninglessness, to fully be present and completely in love, in every task and act of service. To fully be, to bring your full nature and presence into every act of labor, is to become a mountain—to become truly at peace, full of creative power, to know how to truly be alive.

While I am washing a dish, I am living for someone, either myself or the other—and therefore this task is never meaningless. To wash a dish is to take something that is near close to a state of being totally mundane, and rearrange the atoms, to be someone who can do something.

I stare longingly over at the dishes, my invitation to know how to truly be alive, by knowing how to truly be present, meek and strong. *May I know now that meaninglessness can never exist, when I know I am never above a dish.* I am here right now, take me and cleanse me as I wash the dish. Cleanse me of ever thinking I am above the dish, that the dishes are meaningless. That life could ever be meaningless. When I let the dish become meaningless, I let myself become hollow and arrogant. Fill me now with meekness and gratefulness for the occasion of being introduced to the wonder of washing the dish, as the dish washes me.

I've been disappointed by Love.
Cause I've been holding onto this grudge, Love, against
your mysterious ways.
Love won't you come and show me the way out of this hole
I've been digging, since they first came and took my little
voice away.

I've been disappointed by love, the love from a father, the love from a mother, the love from a friend, the love from a lover, the love from God, the love from another, the love from myself, the love from a teacher— I've been disappointed by love. I said it; finally, it is out, no more need for concealing a truth so real and acidic in me. The disappointment eats away inside of me, pulling me out of this world, turning what I see and experience in my external world into a half dream, half real existence permeated by my malaise. This perceived and sometimes overly repeated and felt disappointment, is an experience of disillusionment. I have been disappointed by love. I thought love is the one thing I thought I could always cling to.

Now love, won't you be the one, I call on you to show me the way out of this wasteland of emotional ambivalence, of not knowing if, when and how I will be able to give and receive love again. Lead me out of this real and unlocked dungeon of crushing disappointment, and failed expectations—which likely started from the first unheard midnight cry in infancy, and then on to the shame of rejected an unrequited (unanswered, unreturned, mislabeled) love. So many times I mistake love for my desire to be loved.

Love, take my tiny hand; lead me up the dark and damp cobbled stone steps towards the fresh air of the day above. As I look back I see, there is not even a door to this dungeon, it really is unlocked, and I can freely come and go, from the open-air possibilities of the outside, back into the enclosed dark walls of the dungeon of disappointment. What direction will I move right now, who or what will I trust to guide me through my life? This is a question I must ask and find an answer to.

I am prisoner down there, but I am a wrongly accused prisoner. I have been wrongly accused of believing that I do not deserve this gift, the gift of love. I have been wrongly accused by thinking that there is something I can do to deserve and earn love—and that I can earn and pay my way out of the dungeon. The truth is that the dungeon is not locked and there is not even a prison guard, there is nothing to be paid.

I have been given the gift of life, without ever asking for life, I never asked to be born, and my life was given from a giver, of unknown origins. All our lives have been given to us in this way; I cannot look the giver of life in the eyes and demand a concrete answer. It seems that only the poets, artists and mystics find a way to dig up these answers. The gift of life is a gift of love.

This gift of life was freely given. There is nothing more sacred than a freely given gift, when there is no expectation of returned payment for what has been presented to us. The gift is sacred, because it stands alone in a world that is based on an economy of debt and inequality. The gift levels all social status and privilege, for a gift of love can be given from the least among us and from the ones with ultimate power and status, which then demands us to question what true wealth is. The gift knows no gender and sees no age. Children can give us the greatest gifts of all by the simplicity of their innocence and smile.

Life has been given to us, with no expectation of returned payment. We have been given the gift of ourselves. A gift given like this is a gift given in love, yet I have been disappointed by love, by the gift given, because I have been accused of not deserving this gift of love. I have been accused of not deserving life. I have obeyed a command that this gift is not free, *that my existence is not worthy enough to simply exist and be.*

I have also looked for the gift to be given to me from those who have not yet learned the sacredness of gift giving. Sometimes love is given in a form that is worn out and crumbling at the slightest touch. I am disappointed in this gift, these gifts given by feeble hands and fellow dungeon dwelling prisoners like myself. Oh, how can we get out of this state of not knowing how to receive and give the true gift?

By taking a journey inside the self and trusting that I will find this free gift of life inside. When realizing that my disappointment in love is simply that, just a disappointment, and an accurately expected disappointment. I am not saying the pain and suffering are not real, I am saying, *they are not the only things that are real.* Disappointments are to be expected, families and societies have not been setup to receive and acknowledge the gift yet. The pain and suffering will continue, and the gift will continue inside of us as well— we are the gift freely given.

The gift greets us every single day as we take our first conscious breath in the morning. A gift of life has been given to us, and it has been given with no expectation, except to know that it has been given and given freely. Since this gift has been given to us freely, we have been shown that there is an inherent and infinite value to be found within the self. This value can only be found when the self acknowledges that it is a self, a unique individual, given a unique and one of a kind gift of the self—that we are an unconditional gift.

—

The gift of the self, is a one of a kind gift, never can it be recreated or given again. The economy in this world says that things are priceless when they are one of a kind, and every individual is a one of a kind and priceless gift.

The inherit value placed in every individual given the gift of life, forces the self to either receive or reject this gift—to receive or reject love. We must receive or reject ourselves. We must reject the idea that, we were never have meant to been born, we were born, we were given this gift of life, and we are meant to be.

If we were not meant to be, then we simply would have never have been. There is no way of denying our lives as having meaning, because we are alive, we were meant to be. The question is how will we be, *how will we be found being in this life*, acknowledging the free gift of life, the symbol of love, or remaining in an unlocked dungeon inside the self—hiding ourselves away.

Life is destroyed when it is not seen as the freely given gift of life. When life can be received as the, definitive and fundamental gift, with no strings attached, there is the possibility to love and enjoy life. We must come up out of the dungeon of disappointment and into the free and open air of possibility. Life is always meant to be lived up here, where birds sing songs for nothing more than the enjoyment of singing, and warm breezes kiss our faces reminding us that even nature wants to comfort us. When we come up out of the dungeon and into the open air, we even have the chance to encounter the other, who can freely give the gift to us, as we freely give the gift back to them.

Children have evolved to cling to their caregivers, even cling to the abusive and neglecting parent. Children would many times rather stay with their abuser, over being shown a way out. Children cling to those who have given them life; it has been ingrained in us through evolution. We must cling with this same fervency (not to those who use and abuse us) to something, even when we don't trust life, and that the gift has been given freely and in love, we must cling to the gift of life within us with everything we have.

We also must stop clinging to the disappointment found in conditional love, clinging to the impacts left on us by those who have abused us. We must realize that the gift of love and life has not disappointed us, and it is only those who are too still searching like us for the gift of life inside of them, who have disappointed us. We can have empathy towards those who have hurt us.

I must open up this gift today and recognize my life, who I am, that I have been given the gift of life freely and unconditionally. This is love. We are all gifts, unique and priceless. Treat yourself and every other as such, and love will be fulfilled.

No Shame

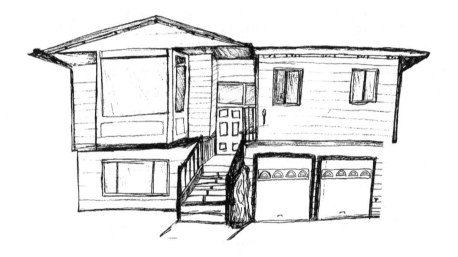

You begin walking through a meadow of knee high grass; you cannot tell if you are walking or you are floating, you are being carried by the softest and warmest breeze. The light is what photographers call the golden hour. Everything is showered in golden light, not too bright; your eyes can take in everything around you. You are neither male nor female; you're past right now is nothing but encouraging memories of inner strength. You find a unique pleasure in every blade of grass, as you pass by they caress you like silk, and have a heaviness that provides the comfort of caring and strong hands. You find a unique pleasure in yourself, as you know you truly do exist, and your existence has become the definition of good.

You find no hours, minutes or seconds here, walking through this grass in the golden light, seems like all there ever was or ever will be. You are totally open to all of this changing or staying the same. A deep inner calling and purpose pull you forward. You raise your arms and move them for the sake of movement. You are totally alone and feel everyone is near you at the same time. The golden grass goes on forever in either direction, an ocean of peace. There is no burden, no weight to carry; your shoulders feel light, like the wings of a bird. Your smile radiates through your whole body, making you feel weightless. You continue walking in the golden grass; warm breezes caress your whole body. There is no nakedness; you are clothed in only you and without shame.

Suddenly, you fall down into a hole, darkness lies before you, you look up and see the light slowly coming to be only a pinhole above your head. You close your eyes as you wait for the weight of your body to crush you when you hit the floor. Death is imminent. You land, but are not crushed or injured. You open your eyes, you are down in a deep cavern, there is light, but no perceivable source, and your eyes simply know how to see in this darkness. Your mind aches, your heart bursts with fear as you remember what you were experiencing above. You've been here before. You sit in silence. You ponder your existence; you are trying to refuse the anger that is welling up in your chest. A weight is now being poured down slowly like lead, molding to the contours of your neck, head and back. Helplessness overtakes you. This weight is unfamiliar, it has not come from me, and it is being poured over me unfairly. Please make it stop.

As you realize the weight has stopped being added on, you decide that now is the time to move and get up. The weight is just the exact amount you can handle, anymore and you would just fall over onto your side or face. You move around in the darkness like a mummy with this liquid lead weight now starting to harden over you. You scream inside your mind, where did this hell come from, who poured this horrible burden and weight on me. I hate you. Take it from me, take me back to the light above, it seems I will never get there now on my own.

We are walking and striving in this chaos of the universe, one moment in the hopes of heaven, the next in the darkest of caverns below, and we are not given a good reason for where we find ourselves. Where does this weight come from, how did I fall into this hole? What is the spiritual journey that I am on? I feel I was meant to fly, grow wings and be free. Then I could fly right of this place, although there is no light to even lead me.

This lead is the weight of work, not the kind of work that earns money, another more nefarious kind. This is the weight of working for an invisible taskmaster, who only commands us *to toil in meaningless* tasks. That taskmaster can never show their face, if they even exist. Some might call this taskmaster the devil.

There is an accuser inside of us. The accuser with no proof of their message repeatedly accuses us of not being enough, spewing lies and accusations across the universe, random arrows flying with no known target. We sometimes are struck down randomly without cause—we forget that we never deserved this arrow, but grow to think we did.

We slowly build this weight of armor up over are bodies, we are weighed down by it, and we think, let the arrows never pierce us again. Yet I am meant to be up there, free, let me grow wings to fly up and out of this. I will close my eyes and put all my attention on this weight now, this burden of living in a world where random arrows fly with no known target. I see this burden now only reminds and mocks me of the golden fields of grass and hopeful expectations above. I still cannot remove the weight. It does not matter. What does matter is that I must cease working for this taskmaster of doing the work of meaninglessness.

Of meaningless striving and serving an invisible taskmaster accusing me of never doing enough, that I will never be enough, that the light of the day by the sun, or stars at night is not enough. I am breathing, thinking, and have the ability to imagine goodness, that is enough. I am here right now and can acknowledge all that has ever happened to me, that is enough. I can choose to want to believe, without feeling it to be true that I am as valuable as anyone that has ever existed, and that is enough. I can decide to believe that I have my own unique face and bodily features that is enough. I can worship a known or unknown God that is enough. I am enough, being alive in full acknowledgement of me and the mystery is enough. I can do all this right now weighed down in this darkness.

I am seeing the pinhole of light appear again above me, is it racing towards me, or am I racing toward the light. Maybe I am growing bigger and bigger and I am starting to fill up the vacuum of this space. I smell fresh air coming in as I get closer and closer to the light. A rush of joy and pleasure releases from my heart into every other felt space in my body. I hear all the joyful moments in my life as I am racing up towards the light. I close and then open my eyes.

You begin walking through a meadow of knee high grass; you cannot tell if you are walking or you are floating, you are being carried by the softest and warmest breeze. The light is what photographers call the golden hour. Everything is showered in golden light, not too bright, so your eyes can take in everything around you. You are neither male nor female; you're past right now is nothing but encouraging memories of inner strength. You find a unique pleasure in every blade of grass, as you pass by they caress you like silk, and have a heaviness that provides the comfort of caring and strong hands. You find a unique pleasure in yourself, as you know you truly do exist, and your existence has become the definition of good.

You find no time here; walking through the grass you see dunes with sea grass blowing in the wind ahead in the golden light. You are totally open to all of this changing or staying the same. A deep inner calling and purpose pulls you forward towards the sound of seagulls and the crashing of the waves. You raise your arms and move them for the sake of movement. You are totally alone and feel everyone is near you at the same time. You find a pathway that has been cut through the sea grass and head up the dune, as the wind kicks up and blows sand against your face. There is no burden, no weight to carry; your shoulders feel light, like the wings of a bird. Your smile radiates through your whole body, making you feel weightless as you reach the top of the dune and stare out as the light is blinding coming over the horizon. The ocean lies before you, all possibilities lie before you. You continue walking down the dune towards the waves; warm breezes caress your whole body. There is no nakedness; you are clothed in only you and without shame.

This sounds too good to be true...this is too good to not be true

Day 11

There is a terror in the middle of the night
I've been running from it my whole life
For the fight against loneliness is like boxing without light
"All of humanity's problems stem from man's inability to
sit quietly in a room alone."
–Blaise Pascal

Come to me now, you who are weary and burdened and I will give you rest, the inner voices speaks to itself. Rest from what, it seems we do not only need rest from a day's work and sweat. We must respond to an internal voice saying rest, yet we run from the inside of ourselves, preferring to be distracted, scared to look inward to find rest. What terrifies us about looking inward, is that looking inward inevitably leads to a feeling we call loneliness. To look inside is to only find and feel ourselves. If we feel alone when we are with ourselves, we must get to know ourselves better, acquaint ourselves with the parts that are unknown and lonely. We must find rest from an impossible burden we carry of loneliness, or a burden of not knowing our self. If we cannot bear to look inside and be with ourselves—then we cannot hear this internal voice calling us to find rest within ourselves.

What is loneliness but the realization that we are the only ones of us, and that there are parts of ourselves that are unreachable and unknowable to others. To truly look inward is to face the singularity of our existence. I want someone to reach inside and touch this dizziness inside me. The more realization we have of our own unique self, the more realization we have to the potential to be utterly unknown and alone. This is the terror that comes in the middle of the night; this is the fight against loneliness—to know the vastness that occupies this space inside our minds.

Now will we continue to run from ourselves forever, fighting against ourselves, or will we take the chance to go inside of ourselves feeling and knowing all of ourselves. Perhaps one of the bravest things a human being can do is to face the self, feeling this sense of being alone inside them, and to do that without wavering and without fear. To be still inside myself, being with the only me, is a strength that cannot be broken, as long as my mind is healthy from disease.

We start off as infants crying out into the darkness, whether we are cold, scared or hungry, we whimper, then we yell out into the darkness, will someone come and help us, there is a need I cannot meet on my own, I need another to come and care for me. No one comes, and so we yell louder and louder, as the instinctual realization of being alone overtakes us, now we are in a fit screaming uncontrollably until someone comes. Maybe someone does come, maybe someone never comes, either way we face a moment of feeling *totally alone* and *helpless* to this reality of the unique subjective self. From the day we are born, we face this battle of loneliness, *of feeling desires within ourselves that we seem unmatched for*, of caring for ourselves alone.

We feel unmatched for loneliness; maybe this is because we start physically attached to someone in the womb. Maybe this separation at birth is something we never quite get over, and we continue to crave this attachment.

Yet I still come to believe that even in physical attachment, there still is the inner reality of the mind and spirit that is always separated and unreachable from the other. This being separated from the other, is a burden we carry of being a unique and subjective self—the only ones of us in the world. We have gathered into families, tribes and empires. We ride on buses; we seek therapists all in this effort to avoid the terror in the middle of the night, in a constant bid to not feel trapped and isolated inside of our minds and bodies. We drink, do drugs and have sex to believe we are having shared powerful experiences, to keep us from feeling and experiencing ourselves. And these experiences can be good and healthy no doubt, and at the end of each of these experiences, there is still ourselves we must face alone inside our mind and body.

To feel your loneliness is to feel that you really do exist, and to have the sudden realization that you are alone is to experience your own unique self, this is actually a moment of true empowering autonomy. Contemplation and transcendence can begin in this moment, if we dare to embrace ourselves. Perhaps when the world feels like nothing more than a dream and unreal, it is because we need to feel how real we are—and this is most felt when being willing to feel our loneliness and uniqueness.

To feel lonely is to be human. If I feel terror in the realization of knowing my existence, then I teeter on the edge of falling into an abyss of despair and insanity. If I tremble at the sight of myself, there is no greater fear and the feeling of being trapped, for I cannot escape myself.

I have walked this edge before, feeling as if my brains were about to implode inside my skull, as I faced the raw reality of existing as a self in a vast universe. I had to call out to "God," from within my mind, "Help me," to save me from this despair. In this moment of calling out from within, peace came. How was this possible, this movement from insanity to a sea of internal peace at the speed of a thought. I am not telling anyone to call out to God, I am telling you what happened to me.

I was lying next to another human being when the process of insanity to peace began, I was not physically alone, I could have reached out and touched somebody and they would have touched me back. I was not reaching for *someone* else; I was reaching out for something inside myself. And when I reached, I can only assume I touched something, this something could only have been myself. I called out in my mind to God, and God did not come into my bedroom, and did not speak back. God did not show up. No words left my mouth, and yet my mind and body returned to a harmonious equilibrium. I reached out to something beyond being trapped by my own loneliness *from within myself*, and found peace. I stopped fighting and boxing, and called out to something inside myself, and something happened. It was not necessarily mystical and it was not religious, it was a shift from fighting to peace, and it began with admitting to myself that I needed something that is beyond myself, and I needed help from within myself.

What can be beyond the self? I cannot think of anything beyond the self, except the self-beyond the self that is residing in the self—I don't even know what that is supposed to mean—except the spirit within. I called out to God, because God represented the idea of there being a purpose an order in the universe, I called out in hope of this idea. I called out because of hope enabling me to call out.

—

Hope is the antidote to this terror of despair. I called out, in spite of finding the terror in the realization of being alive, to something inside of myself. However an individual finds this hope whether in calling out to God or meditation it does not matter. What matters is that a person finds and connects to a hope inside them. The hope is that no matter what, I have come to have life through some sort of order and purpose, and that this is the foundation of being alive. That if I am alive I am not alone, I am with myself, that there is comfort to be found even within the unique and lonely self—that I can accept my loneliness.

The terror is to think that because you are alone and unique, that knowing this reality is particularly scary. That because you came here without asking to be brought here, that there is something wrong with that. If you are here with us right now, than you are supposed to be here, a human being is never a mistake with that simple belief. Whether a person is the product of lust, rape or deep interpersonal partner commitments, if they are here, then the moment they arrive, in that moment it has been decided that they were meant to be here.

We just need to take a moment to welcome ourselves to this life, and to give ourselves a good welcome. When a guest comes to your home, how do you greet them, if you are a good host they will feel at ease and trust you to provide them with what they need? As you let your unique self, come into existence into the reality of your own mind, great yourself as if you are the kindest and most welcoming host.

Wanting yourself to be here, stay, and enjoy your presence. That is right; *we must learn to enjoy our own presence.* When this is not possible to enjoy our own presence, then we must seek out another who can teach us how to enjoy ourselves, when this is not possible then we must take a leap, a wild leap into the world of hope and unconditional love of ourselves, whether we believe or feel it or not. We must take a leap of belief and love ourselves with gentleness. I must welcome myself into this life, so that I become my life.

"All of humanity's problems stem from man's inability to sit quietly in a room alone."
–Blaise Pascal

To doubt oneself is the other death by suicide, an *internal* demise caused by our own judgments and feelings. I want to offer something to life, I want to leave a mark, let my presence be known. When I leave the room, I want the other to feel as if something is missing. When I leave my body, I want that someone's heart feels broken and grieve that something irreplaceable will never come back. I want to be *someone* I say, *as if it were possible for me not to be someone.*

The reality is that I am someone and that is the *truest* thing I can and must know. If I obey the voice of self-doubt or obey the voice of pride that originated in unhealed and unprocessed pain, that is the only time when I fall into jeopardy of not being someone, of not being real.

A child draws stick figures, we put it on the wall, and say thank you for bringing something into the world. The child feels that what is inside is something that is worth offering, I am something and I have something, I am worth being seen and heard. The child knows that their art does not look like it was done by the hands of a master painter, and yet they still see and then feel their value.

A child draws stick figures, and we do not put it on the wall, we point to the fact that it is just stick figures—that there is nothing more special about this stick figure than that other child's stick figure over there. Now I do not want to bring what is inside me out into the world, I do not have anything to offer life. I look inside to see what I have to offer, and I think, I do not have anything to offer. I doubt myself.

A seed of who we are is trying to grow and push its way out of the soil and into the light and air. The seed is hibernating, holding life (a gift) inside of us, what will grow from within us. Will we produce: the beauty that is in a flower, give warmth as in the wood of a tree, or give grain as in bread that sustains life? There are seeds inside of us that have been waiting to push up out of the darkness and into the light of the outer life. We feel something wanting to come out, and we doubt that it will have anything to offer.

The seedling seems so small and fragile, vulnerable to the slightest cold temperature or harsh breeze. I do not want this seed; I hate being vulnerable to mines and other judgments, better to leave the seed dormant. This seedling is inside of me, and I create the environment that the seed will grow in, the only danger is the danger inside the self.

The self-doubt and hatred is the only thing that will cause this seedling to die inside of me time and time again. The full and utter rejection of the self is what causes there to not even be light for the seedling to know which direction to grow towards. Vulnerability removes the lid - that is blocking the light; vulnerability will cause the seed to grow.

I put a hand over my heart and believe that whatever is there will grow. May the hand that I lay upon my heart be a hand that has warmth and compassion, so that the seed feels its warmth and knows it can come out of the dark and into the light. There is never a time in life where this cannot be done. The time is always *right now*; the right time has not already passed us, and will not be waiting for us in the future. The time has to be now, because there is no other beginning that exists except now. Do these actions now, place a warm hand over your heart.

What we have to doubt in the self is the voice of pride that comes from pain. The voice of pride that says I will never let another see me as weak again, and I will only give this gift for me and no one else. We must doubt the seed that grows from pride and seems to grow towards the *light*, but really is just a black hole utterly void of light; it appears only because it takes away all the light around it.

These black holes inside the self leave a weight in our soul (heart and mind) that is so deep that it sucks everything in. The seed that grows from pain seemingly grows up and out into the world, but instead grows inward leaving only a feeling of emptiness and constant dissatisfaction. The gift we give that always leaves us dissatisfied must be questioned.

We do have to take the brave step of doubting this loud voice of insecurity trying to make a name for itself and only itself. This voice is only concerned for self-preservation and image management, which leads to that constant feeling of dissatisfaction and I am never enough.

Go back to the beginning, to that stick figure that needs to be drawn again. Go back to where the self-doubt originated from and see that the voice of self-doubt is not even your own voice. Allow the thing to grow and come out that was done for my own pleasure *and* for the pleasure of the other to enjoy as well. Do the thing that requires some vulnerability and sacrifice, that requires you to move into an unknown, that is what the world needs from us.

We have some unique and familiar seed that wants to grow and offer something to this world. Allow the voice of self-doubt to be silent and see what replaces that voice, what does it say, what does it desire to do.

As I go inward with vulnerability and openness to myself, a single seed turns into a giant redwood tree, faster than I anticipated. A tree that lives a thousand years is now rooted inside of me. The tree gives strength and shelters myself and all who are around me. The tree and I have a depth of wisdom that forms from thousands of years of growth.

This seed is trying to grow and take root in me. Once it starts to grow, self-doubt cannot cut it down. Only the pride that comes from pain can take it down. The voice that says this is all for me and no one else. Just like the pride, that causes the real air pollution and poor ecology in our world, which endangers real material redwoods—so to our pride that comes from pain and past rejection will endanger the good gifts we have inside.

Let my insides and chest loosen from the grip of fear and self-doubt, and allow full and peaceful breaths to come. Do not hide from the stick figures that I doubt are worth something, because self-doubt is like the other suicide, an internal death by my own mind, killing life that is trying to emerge within.

Hope is not a fantasy and fantasy is not hope.
Hope is not a fantasy and fantasy is not hope. Desire is a
fantasy and fantasy is desire. Desire and Fantasy are
always crashing together with fulfillment and
disappointment (this is not to say that desire and fantasy
are inherently wrong).

Hope is not desire and to desire is to not possess
hope. Hope is an ever constant that is not beholden to
anything. To not believe in hope is to believe in a fantasy.
To not believe in the reality of hope that is instigating
chaos into the universe, is to be buried alive trapped in a
wooden box. To call hope a mere fancy fleshless fantasy,
is to speak words into a vacuum of the truest of non-
realities.

I am waiting by the phone desiring it to ring, am I
on your mind as much as you are on my heart. If I burn
with desire bright enough will you feel me wherever you
are and respond? I am sitting in the stillness, all my
inner desire and attention is placed in this waiting for you
to call. If this phone rings it's sound will rapture me in
relief, I will release this desire. I want to release my
desire. I am waiting by the phone and this waiting only
increases my desire to let go of my longing. The phone
eventually rings, and what do I find, but only a stranger
who dialed the wrong number on the other end. Where
are you object of my desire, why won't you call to me?

My heart is now dashed upon the rocks in
disappointment; I curse myself for even thinking to have
hoped for such bliss to come to me. *Hope is not desire and
desire is not to hope.* I curl back inside myself and stand
upon a rock of disillusionment, there is no such thing as
hope—I assume now that to hope is to only build
sandcastles in low tide thinking they could actually last.

Every one of my so-called hopes has eventually been crushed to pieces by the waves of the impending and all-powerful tide of eventuality. This is the actual reality of a life of desire, disappointment; I etch this on the stone tablet of my heart. That is what desire can do; it can turn me heart to stone as it hardens under the constant arrows of failed expectations and unrequited desire. What can soften my heart, it is not desire, it is hope.

Hope can bring my heart back to life and start to beat again, this time with healthy expectations—a healthy expectation for hope. This is because the anticipation of hope is not desire, and therefore can never be disappointed, because hope is an ever constant and never changing reality. Hope is the positive chaos that has been sewn into the fabric of our universe, just wait and see, a tear is about to break open upon us, and hope will come shining through. I must learn the difference between what it means to desire and what it means to hope.

Hope is intrinsic reward. To have hope is to surrender and let down our guard, to let down our guard to what. To let down our guard and disbelief to the constant possibility of finding love, peace, joy, forgiveness, strength, survival against all odds, discovery, meaning, revelation, renewal, redemption, romance, God, friendship, sleep, health, creativity, random smiles, reconnections, spontaneous laughter, new paths, warm breezes, surprise parties, self-acceptance, emerging at any possible moment in our life.

To have hope is to not desire any one thing. To live in hope is a state of mind. When we trust that hope exists, we can continue to position our hearts towards that, constantly pointing our heart towards that warmth. To have hope is to be *open* to allowing something good to come into our life at any possible moment.

To *not* have hope is to reject a part of the reality of life; it is to be closed and locked in, to be at war with possibility. Hope is not a fantasy. To not believe in hope is to give in to a fantasy. To believe in the fantasy of a universe without hope, is to allow de-evolution to reside in our consciousness, and take us farther and farther back to reptile brain. To take us back to a place where only the *one reality of fear exists.*

To de-evolve back to reptile brain is to arrive at a place within us that only knows and trusts our preparations for danger. Reptile brain scurries away from anything that is unknown and attacks even the hand that tries to save it. Reptiles know no hope (I don't judge the reptile as less than). Hope pulls us out from the singular expectation of pending fear, and opens us up to the infinite possibilities of the universe.

I use to build sandcastles on a beach with a loving force in a place far away in time and location from where I sit right now. I use to think that love would come into my life, and I would feel known and strong. I use to wonder and think that one day I would know where to put all the love I hold in my heart. I use to think that someone would accept and know all of me, and all the things that I fear and keep secret. I use to think that one day I would have a gift that I could offer and discover who and what I am.

All of these things have come to pass one way or another in my life, all of them have fulfilled a desire in my heart in one way or another, and all of them have broken my heart in one way or another. None of them was or is the essence of hope, yet hope brought them all into my life. Hope enabled me to be open to receive all of the gifts that are in my life. Hope enabled me to let some of them go. All of them have taught me that hope is waiting to break through and tear open into the fabric of my life. I cannot possess hope, but hope can possess me, if I am vulnerable, open and position my heart towards hope, hope emerges as an internal glow.

Hope is something that is unconditional; it does not even require a believer to make it real. Out of a dark big bang of chaos, emerged a consciousness that became conscious of hope. To even be able to ponder an idea of hope, of all this impossible life around us, is to know that hope exists. To surrender to this very real possibility of good that can come in any instant into our life, is to know hope.

We cannot let our heart freeze under the failed expectations that desire can bring time and time again—we need to disconnect desire from hope. We can be open to the likelihood and possibility of good that is waiting to make its presence known, and to be known even right now as we move our hearts toward the reality of good that is inevitable. We need to allow desire and disappointments to come and pass, and hold on to hope as a reality. Hope is a constant reality based on the possibilities of good, which can and will emerge at any moment.

Good things come to those that wait. We have been taught this concept; I wish I knew where this saying comes from or what it is based in. I have to learn to question the belief; that good things come to those that wait. That only when there is a pleasing ending is a thing worth waiting for.

If we wait long enough, the only thing that is truly coming without a shadow of a doubt is our eventual death—so do good things come to those that wait. I am not making the point that death is the worst thing, I believe living without living is. Is perpetually looking toward the ending and the happy desired results of our current less than desirable situation, where our minds should be trained to go? For we already know what lies at the end of this road.

Western stories and film have tried to convey and reinforce this glorification of the gratifying self-serving ending to our negative life circumstances. Teaching us that a story or movie is only good and fulfilling, when there is a happy conclusion—that we are owed and should except our lives to go as they do on the silver screen.

This belief, that we are owed something good, is the most present and extreme to those in society with the most power and entitlement (presently those who are stereotypical males and light skin toned). Is life really only good if there is a positive resolution to our problems?

Hollywood teaches us to expect something good to happen, that the only reason to keep reading or watching is to wait for this satisfying resolution. We come to believe that we are failures when we are not able to solve and conquer what we deem as bad. Some of us even go so far to think that we have a regretful life, because we are not having storybook endings. Good things can come to those who wait, and the *true good* is not found in the ending.

The real good is found in the waiting itself, not in the resolution or the ending. The building tension is a good thing, it is the event we must push into and receive from. To be totally engaged in the present, and finding the good is in the waiting itself. Like the building up to orgasm, if you cannot deeply focus in on the tension that is intensifying, the release will never be as good.

The more aware and open you are to the tension the better. In fact, if there were no sense of tension, the release would never take place at all. You could argue that the tension and the conflict is the pleasure, that the ending, although it brings relief is not what is felt as pleasurable. Truly experiencing sexual pleasure is being able to maintain and *wait* in the tension. They say good things will happen to those that wait, but really, good things are happening to those who are waiting.

Those who are willing to wait, and be totally involved in the waiting process will receive good things— those who are waiting are receiving good things. The good and best thing is to be engaged in the right now. Those who are willing to stop looking only towards the end are beginning to start to truly live.

Eating for the sole sake of swallowing is not actually eating, it is something else. To look only towards the future is to be stuck. To embrace waiting is to embrace movement and flow. We are only creating in the moment, once the song is written and the picture taken they are frozen in time, to be in the waiting is to be creating. When we are invested and valuing the waiting, we are moving within possibility. Now we are moving away from despair, and moving toward possibility.

To only find yourself being invested in a specific ending is to teeter on a tightrope of despair. To have surmised and concluded that the best possible outcome or heroic ending is all that you will accept, is to crown idealism as king. If idealism is our king, it is just a mummy of despair shrouded in a tomb of gold and jewels, the riches who will benefit neither the dead nor the living. To worship idealism is to believe you are the god of knowledge and experience; it cancels out the mystery and fluidity found in *engaged waiting*. What an ideal ending truly represents is a feeble guess at what we think is best.

If I think deeper, my ideal ending will very well likely end up being a horror for someone else. Someone's daddy might have had to die for this other person's daddy to live. A sudden tragic death brings life to another. This one person's habitat was destroyed, so that that this other person could live in warmth and luxury, and drink good coffee. The mining and deforestation of one person's habitat that will make their culture extinct, is bringing cheap energy to someone else.

When life is thought of in this connected context, there is no such thing as an ideal ending. There are only those who are enjoying the waiting and therefore have become rulers of the moment. A ruler of the moment's authority has not been granted to them from being able to make subjective positive outcomes manifest, but in the power to shed idealism and embrace waiting in the tension of the unknown.

80

Positive outcomes are to be appreciated and are far too often overvalued. To desire a positive ending only tells us that we are normal, and are drawn to the positive and repelled by the negative. Even amoebas' function on this level of simplicity, moving away from what causes distress and towards what supports life. Finding a greater purpose in the waiting does not detract from fulfilled desire.

We should stop focusing only on our positive ideal finales; again, this is not a call to masochism or nihilism. There simply is a contemplative voice calling to be in the waiting, and to shun the idealism of storybook endings. When we value waiting, waiting turns into something else. Waiting becomes us simply living and engaging in our world with creativity and hope.

I have waited a thousand years, and yet still I am waiting

Long ago I know I came to be upon this shore to look upon this sea

I assume for some good reason, a motivation now that I have long forgotten

What is it I have been waiting for all these years?

Was is it a ship, star formation or my illusion of control

Have I been waiting for sleep to come, a prophet?
Or is there something more at work.

I've been waiting until the waiting finally finds me, and what will it find when it finds me waiting?

Will I be bored, filled with anxiousness, callousness to all?

Will I be self-sufficient ignorant of my need to fall?

My mind clears and recognizes something for the first time, the waiting has come and visited me many times before

It has come each and every day of these one thousand years, to see if I am ready,

Ready for what

Ready to stop only focusing on the waiting, and begin living

AN INTERMISSION

If you have read this far and kept at this daily for the past 14 days consecutively or not, then you are almost halfway through with this contemplative experiment. Are you seeing that contemplation is a real thing, that it is a state of being, a state of fully living and experiencing your mind and emotions—a challenge to push into self and accept that you are you, and accept you with a sense of openness and *unconditional* wonder.

Has anything emerged in you that you previously did not know existed before? If this experiment is working than what needs to be emerging is rooted in three realities: love, peace and hope. Patience is another root that is likely taking hold within you. Patience with yourself and the growth process that started in you the moment your first breath took place. Contemplation is allowing you to tap into this growth process and be present while riding these waves. There needs to be patience in contemplation to allow what needs to emerge to emerge.

Self-hatred's voice is hopefully becoming smaller and smaller or even non-existent. Self-hatred cannot exist in true contemplation, contemplation vacuums out all the air self-hatred needs to breathe to survive. At the foundation of contemplation we are showing compassion for ourselves and giving ourselves a chance to be us, without fear of consequences, and sense of the harsh judgments we proclaim on others, and ourselves and preventing us from intimate relationships.

What is it that you want to become in this life? This needs to be the question you are asking yourself by now. This is not so much to say what is it you want to do in this life, and who is it that you simply want to be without doing anything at all.

I believe in contemplation the *what,* and *who* we are is allowed to become a foundation that everything else is built on, and yes, contemplation I believe is a spiritual foundation. So those of us who do not even believe in the existence of a material or non-material spirit, when practicing contemplation move into a more spiritual state of being. There is still benefit to contemplation with or without the language of spirituality. A more spiritual state of being is a depth and unconditional way of being.

It is a depth way of being because the humility in opening ourselves up to the void allows mystery to tantalize our senses, even the atheist all of sudden in contemplation can know the religious experience. I don't say this for the atheist to know or understand, but for anyone who looks down on atheism or atheists as not being able to experience spirit.

I believe while practicing contemplation connections are made from the left, front, back, right and middle part of the brain creating wholeness, especially when paired with mindfulness exercises. Allowing yourself to keep being open to this experience of contemplation, and allowing all possibilities to emerge about who and what you are, facilitates these connections. Starting with the breath, the void, fear, memory, joy and hope.

Has this contemplative experience been traumatic to you in some way? Trauma is the experience of being overtaken by something more powerful than you, trapping you, and forcing you to experience fear and pain you would never choose for yourself. Contemplation in and of itself is not traumatic, and contemplation can shed light onto the traumas that are trapped in our memories and bodies from the past. If contemplation reinforces traumatic memories and feelings, this is a sign that perhaps you need to seek out a professional who is adept in helping an individual release these traumas from their minds and bodies. If there is only trauma in contemplation, then contemplation is speaking to us to resolve this trauma.

Contemplation needs to restore a sense of wholeness and peace at the end of practice, yes there could be fear involved, but that fear needs to be met with a feeling of confidence at the conclusion. Trauma can rob us of this sense of confidence, and if contemplation is turning into agony, then seeking the help of the other is probably necessary, to help you walk through the deep ingrained feelings of fear. There are some things that people cannot face on their own, we need the supportive presence of the other to find the courage within to confront whatever initially took our voice or power away.

Now let us return to contemplative practice with these three words in mind: love, hope and peace. These three concepts exist in the universe, they are real, and they are not just fantasy. If they are not real to us, it is because we have simply not found them, and does not disprove their existence. When practicing contemplation we allow those three things to find us, as much as we are seeking them out as well. Thank you and thank yourself for allowing yourself the opportunity to exist in a way that goes beyond the everyday rituals and into the unknown.

I have already mentioned that Victor Frankl shares how sonar on a ship sends signals to the deep, and waits for the signal to bounce back, to know what lies in the depths below. In contemplation, many times, we send out signals to the depths below within ourselves, and sometimes no signal comes back to us. Victor Frankl says that in this moment, when no answer is given back, is when we know we are addressing the infinite. Let us keep addressing and looking to this infinite space as well, being okay if no answer is given. Contemplation is perhaps the wonder that takes place between us and these infinite spaces within, let what connects us to this void be love, peace and hope.

SUNFLOWERS AND HOMEMADE MOTHER'S DAY CARDS ON
DINING ROOM TABLE. LEARNED THAT AFTER A TREE HAS
BEEN CUT AND ITS WOOD HAS BEEN TURNED INTO ANOTHER
FORM, THAT WOOD WILL WARP TRYING TO RETURN TO ITS
ORIGINAL TREE-FORM. LEARNED THAT LIKE ANTS, THE
SUM OF COLLECTIVE HUMAN POTENTIAL IS GREATER THAN
THE POTENTIAL OF THE INDIVIDUAL. LEARNED THAT
SITTING IN FRONT OF SOMEONE WHO HAS NO DESIRE
TO LIVE MAKES ME WANT TO RUN THE OTHER DIRECTION.
SMILED EAR TO EAR LAST NIGHT WHILE WATCHING AERIALISTS,
ACROBATS AND CLOWNS PERFORM, ALL CULMINATING IN
A CONFESSION OF SHAME AND ENDING IN A DANCE PARTY,
STARTING OFF WITH EVERYONE SINGING, COME AS YOU ARE.

MAY 10, 2015
12:46

WAS BORED AT WORK, WHICH GIVES ME A SENSE
OF DREAD. THERE WAS SUN, MIST, RAIN AND HAIL
TODAY. WAS TALKING TODAY ABOUT TURNING 33
THIS WEEK AND HOW I USE TO FEEL THAT, THAT WAS
GOING TO BE MY MAGIC YEAR. A 69¢ TACO IS
TRUELY A 69¢ TACO. BEEN HAVING SUPER REALISTIC
OTHER DIMENSION TYPE DREAMS, THE PAST WEEK.

MARCH 31, 2015 21:45

FEELINGS OF EXHAUSTION ALL DAY THIS MONDAY. PROLETARIAT PIZZA AND CAFE DELIA
REMIND ME OF WHAT GOOD IS LEFT OF THE AMERICAN SPIRIT IN RAT CITY.
HER LAB RESULTS CAME BACK NEGATIVE, NEED ANOTHER BLOOD TEST
IN TWO WEEKS. SHE IS HOLDING HER BREATH UNDER WATER NOW, WILL
BE SWIMMING SOON. WHEN YOUR THREE YEAR OLD STARTS KISSING
YOUR CHEEK AND EAR MULTIPLE TIMES WHILE SAYING MY LITTLE
CUTIE, MONDAY MORNING EXHAUSTION ENDS IN MONDAY EVENING BLISS.

MARCH 2, 2015
19:43

HAD ONE OF THOSE REALITY CHECKS WHEN, 30 YARDS AHEAD OF
ME WHILE RIDING MY BIKE, SAW A CAR T BONE ANOTHER CAR,
AND ONE CAR DOES A 180° TURN, UP ONTO THE SIDEWALK.
ONE PERSON'S WORST TIMING—IS ANOTHER PERSON'S PERFECT
TIMING. I HAVE A 4-YEAR-OLD NOW, AND SHE HAS BEEN
DISCOVERING HOW GOOD IT FEELS TO LAUGH. FOUND
OUR ROUTE FOR OUR BIKE TOUR TRIP FROM PAULSBO
TO CANNON BEACH. PARTICIPATED IN A CAREER FAIR AT
A MIDDLE SCHOOL, ACTUALLY GAVE ME A LITTLE SENSE OF
PRIDE IN WHAT I DO. BEEN TALKING ABOUT LIMITATIONS,
AND HOW IN YOUTH YOU TRY YOUR BEST WITH ALL YOU GOT
TO DEFY YOUR   LIMITATIONS, BUT IN ADULTHOOD
YOU TRY ALL YOU   CAN TO FIND AND ACCEPT
LIMITATIONS SO   YOU CAN BE FREE. SUMMER
IS HERE, AND   YES THE WEATHER AFFECTS
EVERYTHING.

JUNE 11th, 2015

I am still here. The external world is happening at all times, it is coming at us from all around, whether it is hailing from above or the earth is trembling from below, life is coming at us from all around. The external world is coming at us at all times and it puts us in danger of forgetting that...I am still here, that inside there is a self that is happening independently and in concert with the external.

There are exciting events and dangerous predicaments that both threaten to swallow up and make invisible the inner I—the inner I that exists through and in it all. We must pause in contemplation and feel, hear and know that *we are still here* in and through it all— know the singularity of our inner self, and how we are separate and connected to the external.

Ten stories up at 8:30AM looking out the window alone, I am still here. Questions of, if I will do my work well enough and if what I am about to do is worth even doing—are subtlety and passive aggressively questioning my very existence in this moment. Until I pause in contemplation and know beneath all these thoughts is the essence of me that is still flourishing. I am like a tree with branches moving and blowing in the wind, with its trunk firmly rooted to an infinite depth and core that has sprung up out of a void and mystery. I am rooted in a tangible and knowable self—I am fluid *and* I am unmovable, unshakable.

What I do is not what I am. The confusion a person feels in this daily internal disappearing act of the self, is accomplished in this misunderstanding—the belief that what I do is what I am. When we leave the house and act our way through the day, and then come home and distract ourselves until sleep, this disappearing act can go on indefinitely. Sometimes anxiety and depression are symptoms of the internal self, trying to pull the curtain up on the stage of acting our way through life—asking us to take off the mask and look in the mirror to recognize who we are. Only thinking that what I do is what I am, and getting lost in the act of daily living, is when I feel like something is missing.

We must stop ourselves consciously and with discipline regularly to see that, what I do is what springs up out of the soil of what I am. This discipline of stopping can be contemplation. When the self seems to be constantly disappearing in the midst of the external world coming in and distracting us from us—we must stop the interactions of the internal self with this external world, and ask ourselves, what am I. We must continue in this pause until we know the answer, and hopefully that answer consists of some sense of knowing that I am more than what I do. We must pause long enough for the internal light to shine brighter than the external. Silencing myself by stopping bodily movements, mental ruminations and knowing that I am more than just a thought or a feeling is a steady foundation to build on. I am still here, and what is the I that is still here.

Starting with the idea of there being a, here, we know that here is a place; we are occupying some material space. I am sitting in this chair and filling a void, if I was not here, this chair would be void of my presence. We are here, we are changing the environment in which we occupy, our breath and body heat is changing the space around me, and I am living, breathing, and filling a space. We are physical and we are real and apart of the material world. Our presence and body affect everything around it. We must be connected to our body.

I am still here right now in the space I am occupying. My body exists in this space and I occupy this body. I am nowhere else, I must stop, accept and acknowledge how much my body and I are here right now in this place and be nowhere else—my mind is my body, and I am in this here and now. I must fully be in this here and now.

What is the I that is here right now? There is more than just a body filling a void in a chair. There is an I that is filling the void of a body that is in turn filling the void of material space. The I is quick to form a judgment about itself and all that it is experiencing, this is boring, I am cold, I'm too hungry, I am tired, is this real, will they think I am sexy, I am conflicted, am I worthwhile, am I a friend, will I be trustworthy, who loves me, I have shame, I am not really apart of the tribe, will I be forgotten, am I who I think I am. The capability to judge the internal and the external is more than what makes a self exist. We are more than ego, super-ego and id.

Judgment is just the wind blowing in the branches; it changes by the day, year and decades. For example, I used to hate myself, I use to think too highly of myself, I love myself, and I sometimes accept myself and I feel ashamed of myself all within the passing of a few moments. What I am cannot always be what I judge or perceive myself to be. I am more than my judgmental thoughts.

—
95

Right now in this moment of contemplation I have to take a leap and believe that I will not know what I am truly, until I know what I am is anchored in an I of love, peace and hope. Until a person is anchored in these three ideas, they are perhaps nothing, but a seed blowing in the wind waiting to take root in the fertile soil of love, peace and hope.

I have to think that I do not even want to know myself until I can know myself in these three realities. I would rather act and be unknown to myself until I am rooted there. That until I know I am rooted in peace, hope and love, I am too scared to even look at myself in a mirror—that I am too painful to know myself, when I am not anchored in those three things.

To know that what I am has been formed in unconditional love, and that the gift of life has been given to me without me asking, is to know the self as gift. To know that deep within my mind there is a sea of glass found in meditation and mindfulness is to rise above my reptile brain, to know peace in chaos. To realize that hope exists at all times in all situations waiting to break through is to truly be alive. Peace, hope and love are what make up what I am, and what I find in the, I, of...I am still here.

Everything is right now and I do not want life to be this simple. This current and exact moment holds all things, there is nothing else besides right now, and I am resisting and closing my eyes to this knowledge and simplicity. This very instant contains the entirety of my life and if I am not entirely here in this instant, than I am not fully living. Everything is happening right now; I must stop and participate in everything that is happening. All there is and will be, will proceed forth from right now...from where I am right now. Allow this realization to flood in and fill your internal senses. Contemplation is allowing life to all of a sudden become only right now, and allowing the simplicity of that to be experienced.

Why do most children seem "happier" than adults do? I believe it comes down to simplicity. Their brains and expectations are simply in a more undemanding stage of development that allows them to exist in the now. Children need to live in this stage of simplicity to develop a sense of balance and wellbeing, which can then carry them into adulthood.

This happiness is obviously not true for all children, those who lack love and live in an atmosphere of danger. Those of us who have experienced this type of childhood say things like, I grew up too fast, or I lost my innocence (my simple way of being) at a young age—and I can't remember what my childhood was like. Adults who feel bitterness, anger or superiority over children must question those powerful negative feelings, and learn from a child's simple way of being.

Why don't I want to let everything be right now in this moment, because if this is all there is, than it is too easy and too simple—yet to find ourselves, we must find everything and our whole selves right now, this is a straight forward and not overly complex way of being. Everything is right now, and everything that will be and was, is right now.

Yes, there is always a future to be planned and a loss to be felt, and there is still only one and only one right now—and this one and only right now must be lived. When life becomes painful, that is how we learn to stray from this present moment. We become stuck and marooned on an island of half living, having one foot in the land of the now and one foot in the land of the ghosts. The land of the now is being in the awareness of infinite possibility, and the land of the ghosts is being in a place of despair, clinging to the thought I am doomed—your heart and mind stuck in a past feeling and memory. Coming fully into the present and engaging with yourself is the only way off the island and into movement.

Why say all this except to point out that one of the main causes of not living is because of real pain in the right now. When recognizing and accepting that everything is right now, we can see that we can hold this pain and that we are not as weak and as broken as we perceive ourselves to be. That since everything that can happen is right now, right now there is a possibility that this pain can start to diminish.

Pushing into and holding the pain will be the eventual release of the sorrow. Stopping the pain, through distractions, enables us from being right now and allows the pain to fester, which confuses are perception of reality. By acknowledging that there is only right now, and being able to accept that right now is painful, we step into real life and see our strength grow from grief. This is transformation.

The concept of time takes away from right now being simple. Time seems to always complicate enjoying the moment. Whether that is because we look forward to Friday, dread Sunday or are waiting for our lunch break. If I got rid of the concepts of time, especially increments of time like minutes, hours and days then I would be left with far less anxiety. It doesn't matter whether I know that what is approaching is good, bad or boring, knowing that time is passing takes me out of just being. Removing the total concept of the tracking of time, meaning there is no second, there is no minute and there is no day, frees my mind from running on the treadmill of constant anticipation for what is next. Remove time from my being.

In contemplation I must stop and say, no, to my concept of time. There is no time, there is only engaging in everything that is right now. It sounds something like this, *there is no minute, there is no hour, there is no day, there is no time, there is only now, there is only now, there is only now, everything is right now, I am right now, I am right now*, this is a mantra to be repeated until we know it to be true. Saying no to the taskmaster of time, at least once a day is necessary for our psychological, emotional and spiritual freedom.

If we are willing to accept that everything is right now, and want to engage with the now in spite of pain or boredom...then pause and realize, where am I? What is speaking to me, what is calling to me? What is suddenly more interesting to me? What in my environment is becoming fascinating, a sound outside, an architectural detail or lack thereof, or the sound of my breath? What about me is all of a sudden becoming more real, the weight of my body on a chair, the anxiety I feel in my stomach, or how smiling changes how I actually feel. What is becoming more important to me, where do my priorities shift?

What is it like to accept reality as it is right now; knowing that right now is all there is to be grasped. How long will we let ourselves stay in this moment of being in touch with the reality of everything is right now.

There is no time in contemplation, meditation, mindfulness, falling in love or being totally in the moment of whatever is able to completely capture our attention. It is in these moments when we know that everything is right now that we enter into another way of being.

What is happening in a state of "flow" is truly living and engaging with what is at hand. If a state of peace is going to be achieved, then it can only be achieved in the now, peace is right now, everything is contained right here, right now. All possibilities exist right now, and from that, we must live moving from one moment to the next.

Day 17

How do I know that I am free? What is my definition of freedom? Does freedom even exist? Why does my heart resonate so deeply with the song, Dreamland, performed by Bob Marley and the Wailers?

There is a land I have heard about so far across the sea
To have you on that dreamland would be like heaven to me
And all the glories we'll have them all
We'll live together on that dreamland and have so much fun
We'll count the stars up in the sky
Oh what a time that will be, just wait and see
And surely we'll never die

There is some other place that I perceive myself to not be right now that represents freedom—and is this representation of freedom *the choice* to be me and act like me without limits and shame. In addition, what is truly acting like me, except the ability to freely choose to act from love, peace and hope. How do I know that I am free, how will I know that I am free?

True internal oppression is to *not* know who I am and to do what I do without knowing what drives me. To be influenced by and act from thoughts that are from an external none loving source, is the completion of despair. I have felt the fear in myself and in others of the thought, this is hell, I am already dead and in hell, and for some this life is truly a self-created nightmare or oppression by the cruel ruling powers that be.

It seems again and again that only in contemplation can we find the how to be free, and the autonomous choices that lead to a sense of purpose and limitlessness, within the very real limitations every person is placed in. In contemplation, we can begin to wake up from the nightmare we find ourselves in our waking life.

There is something in the human spirit that will strive against or run from domination, cruelty, oppression and inequality. Living organisms resist pain and negativity. A tree will grow around an obstacle placed near or on top of it; it will never stop growing towards its goal of basking in the light. Human beings move away from whatever is causing them to not grow towards the light, of being and moving in freedom. What light am I trying to grow towards?

What is causing this awareness of not feeling or believing we are free, this awareness of not feeling free of anxiety, self-doubt, sadness and depression? To have the felt sense we can never change who we are, and that the world and universe are static and no possibilities exist. There is oppression and there is freedom.

There is real oppression that varies in degrees of pain, suffering and limitations: a child wants a cookie and is told no, a worker wants a day off and is fired, a person is dehumanized based on the color of their skin, a person is silenced for being seen as female, someone else is told they are perverse, because of how they enjoy having sex with the person they are attracted to, another cannot afford to buy their way into the social class of leisure, health and paid time off. These are the external limitations that we can be born into without our own choice, and cause us to think I am not free.

Whatever our definition of freedom comes to be is the core of who we are, and determines if we are free. Whatever the idea of freedom comes to mean to us, will give our life meaning. Can we live a meaningful life without freedom?

Whatever our definition of freedom is, it certainly cannot have limitations. And the only things in life without limitations are the unconditional things in life, the experiences and acts done without the need for certain conditions to exist to happen. Things without conditions usually exist in the non-material aspect and reality of life. Things like love, peace, hope, wonder, commitment, creativity etc. are usually the unconditional things that cannot be proved or recreated in a science laboratory, yet we know they still exist.

My best friend says that they are free because they are free to love their neighbors; this is a state of being that cannot be limited by their physical conditional limitations. As long as they are living, they are free to love the neighbor. They know they are free when they are choosing to love the neighbor, loving every person that they encounter in their day.

Jacques Ellul believes he is free because he is free to not act in violence towards the other, even when the other does acts of violence against him; this is a commitment to pacifism—a freedom to choose non-violence. When someone strikes him, he does not strike back; he is living in freedom because he can make this decision to live in a commitment to pacifism. It is a decision that is made without conditions, a free choice based on a commitment to pacifism.

We are free when we know what freedom means to us, and this freedom will have to be a freedom to choose and act in an unconditional way. To live our life in such a way that we can find meaning, regardless of the physical and political demographic limitations put on us. Knowing that our purpose, our freedom is tied to something unconditional within, will free us from societal, familial and even our own individual limitations that we put, or are put on us. If I am free, I know I will feel like me. If I am free, I will know who I am.

We are free to explore and know who we are in any moment and situation in life. Perhaps some of us stay up all night in rumination, trying to avoid this reality, of knowing ourselves, terrified of feeling our uniqueness and finding the freedom in that. If there is one moment in all of our day we have this chance to experience ourselves, it is at the end of the day and the first thing in the morning.

The moment when we say goodbye to ourselves before going to sleep and then greet ourselves back into waking reality, is a moment that determines our reality. Did we end our day feeling like we lived, knowing we lived from internal freedom? Are we waking up in the morning knowing who we are and choosing this unconditional way in life--experiencing the peace that comes with internal freedom? When we decide what freedom will mean to us, we can wake up and go to sleep with peace in our minds, stomach and chest.

Victor Frankl illustrates this for us in his book, "Man's Search for Meaning." He says humans have the ability to turn suffering into meaning, to turn tragedy into triumph. That even in the midst of the dehumanizing environment of Nazi concentration camps, the prisoners found ways to be free, by knowing their unconditional reality of choice. They could still be kind, be committed to love, summon laughter and create art, as they transcended the oppression of the external other.

I personally speak from a place of societal given privilege, a privilege I have no right to have. The freedom I am speaking of on this day is not of the societal kind of freedom, but of the internal kind. Contemplation is a reality inside all of us where we can be free, that is not based in external politically given identities (e.g. white, black, Asian, male, female, Latino, non-Latino etc.)

Contemplation carries us across a sea of material limitations, which are the conditions that make it hard to know and feel our internal freedom. Contemplation is a bridge between the unconditional and conditional in this world, and being able to live and move back and forth on that bridge is freedom. We must work for freedom in both the external and internal realities of our world and life.

These words and days of reading are all just contemplation, were just done on a normal day and required nothing unique or special to happen, except just the opening up of the self to contemplate.

Get carried away on a wave of your smile. Close your eyes and slowly start with your face in a flat affect, jaw and face muscles relaxed, not smiling or frowning, and forehead not tense. Now with your eyes closed, slowly start the process of making a smile, raising your eyebrows ever so slightly and pulling your lips and cheeks upward. Follow this process slowly; observe the changes in your face, lips, and corners of your mouth and how this is connected to your heart and emotions. It doesn't matter how slight the feeling of change is, even if it is like a feather resting on your chest, once you feel the meaning of the smile, hold your face in that position, and get carried away on a wave of your smile.

What does it mean to smile, what does it matter if the smile comes from our heart, or from our face to our chest. We can trust our body's reaction even if our heads and hearts are sad. Sadness does not cancel out the reality of the smile. A smile is a smile, and we have meaning.

To focus on the smile means that there can be an absence of fear, and a movement towards the acceptance of the reality of good. People smile even through pain. I see it all the time as a professional mental health therapist working with people who are grieving, severely depressed or reflecting on loss, a smile will sometimes break through, at a slight joke or even at the realization of just how difficult life can be. Somehow people find a way to smile.

This reality amazes me. John Caputo says something to the effect of; somewhere in some far off dark corner of the universe, there is a person who is smiling. That in a practical infinite and dark universe, there is a person smiling for some reason, a person either finding joy, or irony in the face of pain. There is a reality of the smile in the universe, and we can ride this wave of our smile to some place. How can there be a smile!

A smile is only a meaningless face when we do not trust our smile. Yes, we can make a fake smile, but a smile is only fake, because we do not trust our smile. When we close our eyes and slowly make a smile from a flat emotionless face, something really does happen inside of us, if only ever so slightly, we have a point of decision to trust that smile or not.

To trust means to know that a smile is real, it has a meaning that is leading us towards a reality of joyous dissonance. I have read that a smile gives our brain a shot of dopamine and dopamine is what makes us and notifies us of feeling good and at ease. A smile can trick our neurotransmitters into giving us a chemical that feels enjoyable. Yes even though our hearts and thoughts speak sadness, when we smile we give ourselves a chance to ride that smile somewhere. Our smile wants to lead us out being trapped in a state of no possibility of good.

We smile and coo at our babies, trying to lead them to the experience of the smile. We are saying come out of the darkness and towards the light of a smile, we have love to give to you, you are a joy to us, feel this joy you are giving us and let that joy reflect back on to your face, in beautiful reciprocation. We are smiling to bring you out, and into love, with a smile. There is something so human in a smile. A smile is saying there is meaning and joy in our existence, let this smile be what gives you purpose and desire to grow and live. Baby, come smile with us, ride the wave of your smile as I ride the wave of my smile and feel this goodness through and through.

A smile remains just a face when we are not embodying ourselves. A smile feels fake when we are disconnected from our bodies. A smile does mean something, especially when we can physically connect to a smile without letting negative thoughts cloud the feeling. There is no rule in the universe that we ought to smile— and there is a person smiling just for the fun of it, right now, in some dark far off corner of the universe. And this is happening for no reason, except that we can just smile and let that smile resonate on our face, in our hearts and through our minds. We must allow the smile to embody what we are capable of being at all times, and trust what our bodies can do with a smile and the physical reality of what the smile represents. Yes, I can and will smile in contemplation.

Our smile can be our guide right now. A smile can have information that it needs to get across to us today, information that we are unaware of that exists. Where is the wave of my smile leading me? A smile is trying to teach us that hope is not a fantasy; hope is a reality that exists. That is why even in pain and grief, a smile can emerge out of nowhere; hope can emerge out of nowhere. Someone can smile the moment before their death. That is why a smile existing somewhere in a dark far off corner of the universe represents hope, a smile is a teacher of hope emerging slowly and surely.

A smile can be hijacked by sarcasm and jadedness. What a horrible destination we will find ourselves at when our smiles are hijacked by bitterness, and used for a purpose it was never intended for. A smile is not intended for sarcasm. What is jadedness?

To be jaded is when our smile gets hijacked by confusing hope with fantasy and desire, when life never gives us what we want, and we learn to smile at this, to think that is what life is—that living is to never get what we want. It is a violent state to find ourselves in, to have our smile hijacked by the pain of unfulfilled desire and a belief in an existence without the reality of hope. Let hope, simplicity and a belief in purpose return our smiles back to its natural state of being.

A smile is so much simpler than what sarcasm, jadedness and unfulfilled desire can turn us into being. A smile is supposed to be able to stand-alone and be what it is meant to simply be, a smile. To be a simple-smile that is pulling a baby out of not being seen and into the face of someone that loves them.

Sometimes we have to smile at ourselves, at our own reflection, we have to smile at ourselves and pull ourselves out of the darkness and into the face of someone that loves and appreciates the person they are looking at in the mirror.

Sometimes in our reality, children are born in completely unloving families where no one smiles at them, although I believe this is rare. Even children in this situation still might have the chance of strangers on the street smiling at them bringing them to the reality of the smile. Even a teacher in a classroom or a bus driver will smile at us, bringing us out and into something—if we will just learn to ride and trust the wave of the smile and where it is leading us.

Close your eyes and let your face come to a natural resting position, not smiling or frowning. Now slowly start to make your face into a smile, and hold that smile until you feel your body respond to yourself in a positive way. Let that smile and feeling inform you of the simplicity of hope, of the reality that you are that one smiling in a far off distant corner of the universe right now, representing something far bigger and more mysterious than yourself. Allow yourself to become a participant in this simplicity of your smile. Smile at someone else in simple acceptance of who the stranger is, and receive this same kindness back unto yourself when they smile at you.

Day 19

You are what you love, not what loves you.
-   Charlie Kaufman

You, singular you, you are real, you take up space, you respond to and direct energy that affects the space around and inside of you. You are singular, although made up of many parts and realities, those parts and realities emerge to create you. Right now if you quite all the parts of your external and internal realities, who and what do you find is the singular being that is interacting with the external and internal world? In this stillness what and who do you realize you love, and in this loving, who are you being and becoming? In performing these acts of love what or who are you acting like? Take some time of stillness now with these questions.

Love is commitment, devotion, a fleeting and all-consuming feeling and faith in the absurd—or to say otherwise, the absurd is putting your trust and hope in an unknowable future that may or may not come. To love is to put yourself into and devote yourself to something that may destroy or resurrect you—to risk living and loving in a destructive or life giving way. We are what we are devoted to. What and who are you committed to?

It does not matter why we are, it matters that we are fully conscious of who and what we are living for, or not living for. The who and what we are not living for has just as much impact on us, as to the who and what we are devoting our lives to. Let this knowledge emerge and reverberate in your body and mind. What do you feel when you look at this person you live for and with, is it love? What do you feel when you put your mind and hands to work on this project, is it purpose and visceral? Does what you love support you in return; whether in giving meaning or actual felt physical and emotional love and support? If it is not returning anything but void and pain, why are you committed to loving pain and the void, what purpose does it serve?

What is your experience of life like while you are loving this person or thing, what are the qualities and characteristics of your love? By continuing to love this object where do you think you will end up, is the love you are giving for personal secondary gain, or because the love is the means to the end.

If the loving is a means to an end, than we will never fail at love, we will have already understood the whole of what makes up the human universe. This is to own our love, to embody love. When this occurs, we will have understood what it means to live in love, understood what life means to live at all.

If we are loving for some secondary selfish gain, trying to find our value in another's judgment of our worth, trying to steal their love for our own, this will go on and on and on and on in failed expectations and disappointments—until we find out what life can be when we learn to have love that is our own, and what it means to freely give our unconditional love to others. We are what we love, not what loves us.

Is the glass half empty or half full, this is a perspective question, either way there is emptiness and there is fullness. There cannot be one without the other; the half empty part needs the half-full part to exist. Is there love in you or is there not, if there is emptiness, there is likely love that is shining light on that emptiness. Perhaps a love that was once full inside of you has drained and caused a void of loneliness. To get the love back you have to give yourself the chance and permission to let love in again. If the glass is half-full of love, but all you see is the emptiness, this could be because you are focused on a love that was in the past. Yet underneath this void of emptiness is a glass half full of love, just waiting to be called and named appropriately.

What is right in front of you to love right now, this is the only way we can get in touch with the love that is here right now. The glass if half-empty, the void's reign is present and we wait for a past love to return or in anticipation of a love to come. We must say no to this and find what we can love today, right now. What we decide to love right now is who we are. Do we love ourselves, than we are at peace and moving toward health? Do we love our child than we are a parent, sowing seeds of patience and strength for later use in that person's life? Do we love our friends, than we are connected and not alone in this world? Do we love our work, than we are not bored and are increasing our ability and engagement with challenge and growth?

When we only see ourselves valuable by judging what loves us, than we are passive empty corpses. We are lifeless cold and motionless on the morgue table, just waiting for someone to give us life, a prisoner inside our bodies and minds. If we are only what loves us, than our internal being has already left us, and we cannot move unless someone makes us move. We feel without a self.

We have become helpless and depressed when we are what loves us. We can be arrogant when we are what loves us, thinking that we deserve love, without thinking we need to own and give love freely and unconditionally too. When we are what loves us we remain in separation from the world at large around us, never truly and fully able to connect and integrate with Reality.

Love is movement and love is patient. Love is patient because it never runs out and always has the time to keep giving. Right now, we have the chance to love today. Life is constantly inviting us to find love. In the apparent meaninglessness of everything, we have the choice to become and choose love. In one of the most followed religions in the world there is a scripture that says, God is love, or that the highest knowledge, power, and being consists, exists and is made of love.

The foundation, repetition and question of this contemplative exercise today is, what is my relationship with love, do I love, love. Are we committed to the absurdity of being committed to something or anything at all? What is our gut response to love and being committed to love? Are we saying we are a fool to live this way, a fool to love this way? If we believe, we are fools, than really we have simply been fooled. And more than likely we were just fooled by the idea that to love means to not feel pain. Once the acceptance of the reality of love is to feel pain is integrated into us, then we are not fools, we have the chance to be truly grounded in something authentic. We are what we love.

And yet another day of contemplation begins and awaits me—I say this with a tone of drudgery, as if contemplation has become a chore. I am suspicious of myself as well. I feel a pressure to believe and feel that contemplation has worn itself out by now; it is time to throw it away and await the next new and novel thing that will interest me and tantalize my senses.

Contemplation has overstayed their welcome, time for you to leave, here is the door, do not call me, I will call you. Consumerist society has created my reality to not believe in anything that could last perpetually, or perhaps believe and value anything that is *free* and comes spontaneously from the self. Perhaps this runs so deep as to think that anything from the self and is internally produced is not as valuable as what I can buy.

The idea that something can last a lifetime puts the whole foundation of our infrastructure at risk of collapsing, nothing can last forever, it must be consumed, used, worn out to perceived obsolescence, and then the new and better is sought after, and purchased.

Contemplation always awaits me, is always there to hold me and lead me into my internal being, and this internal path is a doorway that ultimately leads to the engagement with my external reality. And it is an engagement not as a consumer, but as a viewer, giver and participant.

As I go through the internal doorway of contemplation, I begin to find a way of being with the external that is the embodiment of peace, hope and love. Now only if I will allow myself the permission to not get bored of contemplation, to not allow myself mistrust this always unknown undertaking.

This new contemplative day at first seemed out of reach, and now I have already allowed my mind to be taken hold of my internal self. My internal world seemed so out of reach, and now I have already let myself take hold of my contemplation. I have taken a leap of faith, to trust that when I stepped out into the unknown of seeking something more than consumerist reality that I would land on something solid. I took a leap of faith to feel the internal me, and trust I would find something transcendent beyond the state of the world's affairs, weather and distaste or joy of my work. I am willing to be intricately connected today to my internal self, and all that might await me.

In my contemplation I am willing to block out all external messages that tell me my existence is meaningless without this title or object, that I must perform and act to my societies expectations of my biological sex, and to the implicit messages that I am never enough. Contemplation wants to be the antidote against existential angst and dread. When existential angst is coming from the external, contemplation blocks the chaos of meaningless that shoots at us from the great unknown. When these past arrows of meaninglessness that shoot out of the void have been lodged in us, we seem to be the shooter, from the internal void aiming at the heart of who we are.

In contemplation today, taking another chance at giving our being a shot at transcendence, we can remove the arrow and protect ourselves from the lies of messages that communicate worthlessness to us. We can enter the void knowing that the arrows are only the stories we tell ourselves about ourselves, and not fixed realities. Yet, I am still growing weary of contemplation.

I do not want to trust that contemplation is worthy of my time. I do not want to have to take the personal risk that I will realize that I am not worthwhile, that my internal self that is ready to be discovered and trusted, is nothing special or unique. I feel pain, the pain of this, and contemplation does not allow me to stop myself from feeling my pain, contemplation does not stop me from feeling myself. If I contemplate, I have to be aware of what troubles me. When I practice contemplation, I am aware that I am troubled. Contemplation brings to awareness that I have to be silent with me, and the uneasy parts of me. I have to trust the silence inside myself as an acceptable way to exist. Even in silence, I exist.

This is a day I thought contemplation is done with me. Today I thought that contemplation was bored of me. I felt that I was not interesting enough to engage myself in this way, to engage with the internal me. Maybe when we refuse to engage with ourselves in this way of being, we are really just thinking that we are of no interest, that we are boring. That when we separate ourselves from what we are doing and who we are with, that means we are nothing and of no interest.

And yet contemplation is an invitation to seeing the wonder of who we are, in light of just being alive—that in just being conscious we have something of interest to others and ourselves. In engaging with ourselves fully, we are able to discover the purity of who we are and what we want to be, apart from the messaging of consumerist and human *doing* society. In contemplation, we have the invitation to be more than just human doings, and be human *beings*.

Today is another day that contemplation exists. We exist, we are being. We are so into just being, that we don't even have to control our heartbeat, breathing, digestion, energy production etc. there are parts of ourselves that just are, and we readily accept these parts, we don't ask them anything, or criticize them, they just are.

In meditation a lot of us start with the breath, it is a simple act that we typically do not have to agree with, and in meditation, we start to learn how to participate with this simple act of living and being. We let go and follow the in and out of our breath allowing ourselves to just be. Contemplation exists in the same way, we allow our self to exist in a simple way, as simple as breathing. Allow your inner self to just be without judgment.

Contemplation does not need to be a checklist item, because there is no work to be done in contemplation. In contemplation there needs to be the ceasing of work and the emergence of being. In contemplation, the human being emerges separate from the human doer. External and internal judgment start to die down, and the internal voice and self are allowed to come out and be, and then take in all that exists in the external.

Trust emerges in this state, trusting the self and who we are, which leads to peace. Peace that comes from knowing that we are enough, the ceasing of the battle of thinking we are only a human being by what we are doing. In this peace, contemplation takes hold of us.

Day 21

Is a dream a lie if it don't come true or is it something
worse
-Bruce Springsteen

Am I a lie if what I want does not happen, or Am I
something worse? If what I want is who I am, then I
better know who I am and what I want. If I am not what
I want, and what I want is not coming from who I am,
than I am a false self—the something worse. If I believe,
what I want is a lie, even if it is or is not a lie I become
split in two, in a perfect frozen dissonance. The *if* will
either keep me frozen or will push me into movement and
being real and authentic—either way I must contemplate
the true and the false self and their origins.

A dream is to see, feel, hear and experience
possibility through imagining an alternate reality.
Dreaming is a high calling. Dreaming in its worst form
can simply be a product of privilege that is allowed to
emerge after our simple basic survival needs have already
been met, and at its best dreaming is the spiritual inside
us turning tragedy into triumph. The individual in
privilege and in destitution, both dream.

The call of dreaming is a calling to be a self,
because in each individual's unique dream emerges a
subjective one of a kind self, the chance to be a self. To
contemplate one's dreams is to dissect and learn how the
self forms and works.

The dream that does not come true could be a false dream that should never be allowed to come true, lest that person lose themselves forever in a false dream, if being able to lose yourself forever is even possible. The dream that does not come true could actually be the true self, drawing an individual out into the world to express their unique being, defending the self from the false self. For as soon as the true self emerges, the false self disappears into the blackness of the void. Our failed dreams could actually be us waking up from a nightmare; we didn't even know we were having. We must dream and allow those dreams to speak to us in the moments of silent contemplation.

The false self, the self that has to create itself and project itself outward and inward, is many times what feels safe and what others believe or we deem as good enough. The false self *is* the something worse. The false self ceases to keep growing, and is fixed, and leaves us with feelings of emptiness, an outward shell with nothing in the middle. The false self is birthed in the fear of rejection that is perceived and real. The false self is scared of the dream not coming true, because the false self thinks dreams *have to* come true, therefore the false self cannot truly dream, because it is not open to seeing, feeling, hearing and experiencing possibility through imagining alternate realities. The false self is stuck in the dreams that do not come true, whereas the true self does not stay frozen in disappointment.

The true self bears the weight of dreams not coming true and coming true. The true self dreams and engages with our internal and external life regardless of dreams coming true or not, it is in the dreaming that the true self emerges. Imagining alternate realities is the point. The false self-doubts the dream, the fear of disappointment tells you not to dream, to live in a fixed state of being, to not trust growth and engaging in your life in new ways.

The simplistic theory of adaptation, which is the foundation of biology, teaches us that what adapts survives and thrives. Springsteen's, *is something worse*, is the ceasing of dreaming by the emergence of the false self that is always stuck in the heartbreak of unfulfilled desire, and rejection of our ability to embrace our limitations.

The true self emerges in the freedom to dream without pretense of success or failure. Dreaming can then simply be thought of as, holding to the belief in possibility always existing. Real dreaming is dreaming without fear of dreaming. Dreaming without the fear of unfulfilled dreams, allows the true self to always be developing through engaging with life through dreaming.

In contemplation, it is not about following your dreams, as much as it is about allowing dreams to spontaneously emerge. In contemplation, we have the chance to engage true dreams and true self.

THERE ARE NARCISSISTIC DREAMS AND BORROWED DREAMS...WHAT ARE *MY* DREAMS, AND AM I STILL DREAMING?

Just below the skin, and under my chest bone, in the halfway point between where the bottom of my chest bone and stomach converge lies a longing. This longing is found in a place that is guarded only halfway by the shield of my breastbone, and is totally halfway exposed to many external dangers. When this area of my body is hit with just the right amount of force, the wind will be knocked out of me and I will be gasping for air, as if I am about to die, left totally helpless and vulnerable.

The longing that resides here has a magnitude that carries such a weight, and it is able to cloud my entire subjective universe. This longing in an instant, when revealed, can turn everything in my world to gray—and to think it is only sheltered by 2mm of skin and a small piece of bone. I must know the vulnerability and the strength that surrounds this place, where life and longing exist, just below the surface of the skin.

In our gut, we have the sense of our vitality, life force, and "the core" of us. This place seems to acknowledge the weight of our grief, the excitement of romantic love, and can buzz with existential nervousness at the constant possibility of chaos occurring in our life. The longing felt in this place when embodied, will push us towards spiritual growth.

Allowing that place to become bare and open, lifting the lid back, can send waves of emotion—a mixture of fear and hope. All the same, whether negative or positive feelings come, this place does need to be experienced, lived from, heard and then responded to, or for some, reckoned with.

Some of us will have to reckon with the need to be able to be stimulated all the time, and instead find the awe in simplicity. To find interest and pleasure in the external parts of our reality, that is just happening without any effort on our part. See how the clouds *just are* and how they form different shapes and move without our effort. To be inspired by the gracefulness of our slow and rhythmic breathing. To allow ourselves to notice how the light will shift, shade and color the room we inhabit. How the birds will sing on their own, creating an unknown music to our ears. Consider the sunset and sunrise. How can we participate in all these things that are just happening externally on their own without our help? Can we let the outside and natural beauty of our world just be a wonder, and recognize this in all its simplicity right now?

My spiritual growth and longing will cause me to recognize and seek out beauty, or those things that stir me to experience wonder. To all of a sudden be struck by the mystery of all that is around me. Whether something is manmade or not, there is a mystery to the symmetry of architecture, to the ergonomics of a chair, of how electricity is being harnessed, stored and sent through wires and used to power a life support system and at the same time charging an electric toothbrush. In my spiritual growth and longing, I will begin to see all this, seeking to find the wonder and beauty that is around me. And in recognizing these realities, I will fulfill a *longing in my spirit*.

Now that I can find beauty in my external world, I now need to engage and touch this external world beyond myself. This spiritual awareness does not just stop and take place within the 2mm of skin; it energizes movement to engage with the outside world.

What is the result of all self-actualization, it is the person who recognizes themselves as selves, and can then move freely into the world giving unconditionally and receiving unconditionally. And of course, the height of all unconditional experience is unconditional love, the ultimate human goal, perhaps the fundamental subconscious message.

This movement is not done in ignorance of the dangers of trauma that we will inevitably encounter. It is simply that in our spiritual engagement with longing, we proceed in the knowledge of being willing to accept and know both sides of engaging with what is outside of ourselves, that there will be pain and joy. We become willing to engage with the external, because as we engage with the mystery within and learn to face the degrees of distress this causes us, we become more willing to engage with the external mystery of the other.

The way out is in, and sometimes the way in is out—acknowledging the beauty surrounding us will lead us to our spirit within that is waiting to fill us with transcendent awareness, and in this simultaneous acknowledgment, immediately we begin to engage the external within the shelter of a contemplative experience.

To bring this all back to the center, what is spiritual longing except and awareness of me. Spiritual longing is the awareness of our core self, this awareness is an experience that we alone can only have, we are alone in the experience or our core self, and that is okay.

What is it like to be me, to inhabit my body, fear my fears, remember my memories and figure out what to do with my desires? How will I deal with this experience of being me? Will I decide to deaden my felt sense of me with distraction or substances?

When we are spiritually longing, we are longing to be ourselves alone, to know ourselves as totally separate **and** supremely connected to the external. If I refuse to acknowledge and feel me, and this spiritual longing, then I am unable to find *my* way in a life that is my *own* to own, and my *own* to *share and receive.*

I have to receive my life from the external, since I did not ask to be created, and my way of coming into being was based on others actions and decisions. I must make peace with coming into being, and peace will only come if I trust I came into being based in love and goodness, regardless of the external conditions of my family of origin or culture of origin. This peace will come once I see that I am me, that I am a product of the external and that I now have a spirit that is longing to be me. We are a collective and we are individualistic.

In contemplation today, I engage with this longing within. In contemplation, I am aware of this longing within. Through contemplation, I become myself, and that self is spiritual, because there is uniqueness and a one of a kind self that resides within this body. I must not dampen the longing or criticize my longing by another name like, boredom, loneliness or existential angst.

This is what I feel like when I have a longing, and I am good

This is what I feel like when I have a longing, and I am good

This is what I feel like when I have a longing, and I am good

This is what I feel like when I have a longing, and I am good

This is what I feel like when I have a longing, and I am good

This is what I feel like when I have a longing, and I am good

This is what I feel like when I have a longing, and I am good.

This is what I feel like when I have a longing, and I am good

This is what I feel like when I have a longing, and I am good

This is what I feel like when I have a longing, and I am good

This is what I feel like when I have a longing, and I am good

This is what I feel like when I have a longing, and I am good

This is what I feel like when I have a longing, and I am good

If I give the gift that I never got, then suddenly, I have that gift that I did not receive the moment I start giving. Unexpectedly a gift emerges out of what was once a void, something unconditionally given has now appeared from this nothingness. This something is unconditional because it arose out of a void, out of a place with no conditions, except the condition of emptiness. So to the universe came to be in this same reality, the universe came spoken or banged into existence out of nothingness. I came out of nothingness, yes there was an egg and sperm, two conditions, but in the moment before their meeting, in the middle of those two cells, was a void and in their meeting came me. I can fill the void in me by giving to others and myself.

Yes, it is ok to learn how to trust and give from nothingness without reason to trust this truly spiritual movement and grace. For if we came into being out of a space of nothingness, where the conditional and the unconditional meet, perhaps right now this is where all true new life, growth and movement continues to occur in our lives.

If I have lacked love in my life and I decide to extend love, whether in an act of true altruism or not, I then possess love in that moment. To love is to have love. If I have felt judgment and only valued by what I have to offer, and I then extend grace to another, than I have received and experienced grace transmuted to myself, in the same moment. Where is all this giving out of our own void leading, except to finding community and eradicating loneliness within the self and within our society? Yet this pain and shame of the things we have not received when we needed them most keeps us in seclusion.

Things I did not get when I needed them most turns into a heavy gravitational pull of shame, that keeps me in a cycle, an orbit, around a darkness that is unknown, and I can never quite seem to escape. And when I decide to make the choice to give unconditionally to the other what I did not receive, or give that same gift to myself, then I have this thing suddenly, and my shame turns into strength—and a gift that is given and can never be taken back. I have discovered that I am more than just my pain and shame.

How can this gift emerge from nothingness? I imagine this is what causes us to have the experience and reliance on the saying, blind trust. That sometimes we have to accept realities that are not based in our known perceptions, personal histories, and current experiences and conditions. That our implicit biases that control our view about us, the other, and the universe are not always accurate. That out of our inner silence, nothingness and through facing the void, true change and courage emerges.

I have to stop relying on my pain as the only voice and truth about myself. The voice of shame is rooted in a reality that is no more, the only reality shame can thrive in, is in our repetitive memory loops. I have to know that an unconditional gift, when it emerges is what gives us wings to fly out of the labyrinth of shame every time. And I have to be willing to accept the invitation to take part in a gift that will require a blind unbiased trust.

This act is not as difficult as it might seem, it is as difficult as we make it to be. Accepting the invitation is just like how we let go of consciousness to fall asleep. We have to realize that what we resist persists. We have to let go of the past to receive the new.

We have to be aware that the invitation is being given, to accept stepping into and allowing the gift to come out of nothing. When I give what I never got and needed, or when I decide to give out my place of shame, or from the void I feel as nothingness, I have a chance to resurrect myself out of past shame. I have a chance to find myself in authenticity.

The other story that emerges from this giving of self in this unconditional way can end in a narrative of perpetually never receiving from the other. Yes, I can give out of my void and shame and receive the support and love I have needed from within myself, this is a firm prescription to leading an enjoyable life. And yet I can give and give, and never allow the void to be filled by the other as well.

With this being said, I have to question myself and think, is this just another way of protecting myself from emptiness and fear of the void—a way to keep the other out and from exposing myself. To continually give to others as an act of hiding the shame of my fear of rejection, so as to never experience reciprocal intimacy. As bold as it is to give freely, perhaps the bolder move is to accept the gift freely from the other as well.

How do I let the other give to me and allow them to touch me, except by exposing me, and being the real me with the other. I am only getting one side of all this giving of gifts, when I am the only one allowed to give. The other side is the other giving to me and me being in relation with the other, deepening my experience of myself with them, in mutually giving and receiving. In the same way that it takes two to make a human life, my human story continues with me interacting with another outside myself, to have life continuing to spring and well up in me, in an open connection.

The sting of pain left from the other, causes me to have to learn and grow to see how to give unconditionally and find those gifts emerging inside me. Now that I know this is a choice I can make, of how to give the unconditional gift, I can begin to allow the other to give back to me, without the fear of total annihilation of myself. I am not afraid of the other's love toward me, and I am not afraid of the void in me.

Either way, whether I am giving or receiving, this all plays together in having to relate to the other and myself. I need to be active and engaging in my life. So what are the things that I need to give and receive unconditionally today in an act of blind trust: love, peace, compassion, grace, forgiveness, a second chance, generosity, hope, reflective listening, a smile, a meal, undivided attention, am I hearing this invitation?

When there is only an awareness of consciousness work ceases, and we must cease from work at times. When achieving only an awareness of consciousness that is separated from the words that create thoughts and judgments, meditation begins. When thoughts become just a part of the reality of consciousness and not the main reality, possibility begins. When thoughts are not the only source of finding and creating a self, who we fully are, becomes known. When consciousness is aware of being the separateness and connectedness from words, a self solidifies and a void is uncovered.

If we can stomach standing in front of the void of nothingness our spirit begins to grow. Now we see clearly that, like a black hole emitting signals, our thoughts emerge into understandings; thoughts emerge out of the void of the self. Also, thoughts emerge out of somewhere else, out of places of fear, places that are wounded and superego judgments. Part of contemplation is allowing thoughts to cease, work to cease, time to cease as we wait upon the precipice of the void of nothingness.

There was a time in our life when words meant nothing; they were sounds like waves crashing on the shore, and they held no meaning. In infancy we were beings that were swaddled, tired, hungry and held, and that was our awareness, total body awareness of ourselves, and what held or did not hold us. We trusted those sensations alone. We were only ourselves and were, seemingly effortless in simplicity.

Words began to enter consciousness; thought began to form, and created confusion and self-shaming. We left the effortlessness of the body and entered the endless maze of thought, and the unbearable burden of asking the perpetual question of why. When we escape from the tyranny of our words, ruminations, judgments, and return to the body and simple awareness of consciousness—we escape work, and enter into being. This is not implying that we have to empty the mind of thought; it is that we have to contact the void of nothingness that thought is coming out of, the place where it seems there is no thoughts.

Besides thought what am I most conscious of? The buzzing in my stomach, the heaviness of my head, the stillness in my heart, the boredom in my legs, the tension in my jaw, the temperature on my face. Beyond the body, going deeper into awareness what will emerge into consciousness. What is dangling above the void of the self within, does what is there even matter? What am I projecting over the void within? Am I stealing from my external world, looking to societal and archetypal images, and placing an image of someone else over the void, in order to not face the mystery of me? How often and how open will I be to simply face myself in the actual mirror (bathroom mirror) of the material world and the inner mirror of my subjective self?

Where are all these thoughts coming from, how do I choose which thought to begin to trust and say is me. Do my thoughts even have to be me? The will inside that chooses, is the one that I am working at being. The will that chooses, is not a thought, I am not a thought, I am continually in the creation of movement internally and externally. I am a will of spirit. I am a well full of spirit, there is a well inside that seems to have no bottom, yet continually emerges overflowing with willfulness.

My thought is not the spirit; the spirit chooses the thought and wears the thought as a manifestation of the self. And yet the thoughts come out of a void within, and from the external world that influences the mind of the self—all of the dissonant thoughts that must be taken, and not taken seriously at all. Every thought could be *the truth* and every thought could be a devil. And yet the will that is choosing within, is where the real experience of being a self emerges. I am still puzzled by all of this right now.

Contemplation is a listening of thought, an inspection and deconstruction of thought, through the will of the spirit within—through the life force within. There first must be an awareness of the void and how my will is separated from thought, and then progression can begin.

In contemplation, thoughts can be laid to waste, tried on and manifested into a being of peace, love and hope. If only we would give ourselves a chance to allow a voice to come out of the void of ourselves, rather than grabbing the voices and commands given from the external. Being able to reflect upon everything from a peace within is an act of contemplation.

There is a tyranny of thought. The mind loves to be ruled by thoughts. And in this
silence..
....
....
....
....
....
....
....
........in that space is where life begins. Life does not begin in thought, but out of what emergence in silence. And yet all the words on this page are thought, wars are started and hearts are broken, all by words and thoughts. Thoughts are our stories our memories and how we process our inner experience. Thoughts are of great consequence and are essential. And the tyranny of thought must stop for contemplation to begin and transformation to renew us.

There is wisdom in instrumental music. Listen to an instrumental piece, and allow thoughts to move away, and let the waves of sound move consciousness inside. Experience the awareness of being without thought, and only the observance and movement within. Music without words reflects this other way of contemplation without thought.

Contemplation contains thought and is dependent on the absence of thought. Contemplation is the overlapping of awareness of the void, the thoughts that emerge from within the void of the self, and calling out our projections taken from the archetypal onto ourselves. At the very least contemplation is the attempt of removing these projections of the archetypal and entering a void of self.

"If only someone/thing would just give me the answer and tell me what to do, then I would be okay (not be responsible for my freedom)"
-Every Human Being at Some Point in Time

An answer will always come. Within the most surrealist of dreams there is an answer, hidden in plain view, there is a driving motivation or response to a question. Our dreams are bombarded with distractions and redirections—all of which are moving the viewer and the participant, who within the dream are the same person, in a dance of complete helplessness and autonomy.

We are experiencing three conditions in our consciousness: we are totally autonomous, totally dependent on our environment and totally helpless all at the same time, this is the experience of having subjective consciousness. There is an answer in plain view, and the answer can seem to always evade us. And an answer will always come, when there is an ongoing search for authenticity within the self, and within this space of authenticity is found a peaceful autonomous movement that somehow can coexist with our external conditions. I must recognize this difficulty while still valuing the search for authenticity, to begin becoming a self and enjoying my life.

An authentic answer will always come. What is this search for authenticity? Authenticity is what weathers a storm; it is the 100,000-year-old boulder on the beach that although is worn down by the wind and the waves, continues to be a boulder despite the external conditions.

What is anxiety? Except the external and internal pressure crashing down on my authenticity, and getting lost underneath those waves. When I pause and take note of all that is crashing in, whether through mindfulness or contemplation, and find my authenticity, I am kept above the waves. When the tide comes in and covers over, I still have a place to stand. I am 300 yards off shore, wind and waves pouring down on me, while still standing on something unseen, appearing to hover over the water, never being knocked down. There is room for me in the middle of the storm. Authenticity is emerging. Let authenticity be my desire and search, and what I stand upon.

The surrealism of the dream is a more accurate representation of the feeling we experience of the very real chaos in the material world and our waking lives. Within this chaos, we want an answer, and a tangible authority, an authority that will give us rest inside the eye of the storm. An authority will come that will bring us rest.

Will this authority that takes hold of us be the authenticity of our true selves, a religious dogma, the effects of past trauma that leaves us stuck in negative repetitions of a time that has already past, or the weight of a paternal guilt within the mind and soul that chains us to someone else? The authority of the authentic self is what I find gives me the most peaceful movement.

Within the redirections and distractions of our dreams and waking life, there is an answer and a motivator, a driving force of fear, love, hope or despair— and there is an eye in the storm of all of this chaos. Chaos is the confusion and bombardment from the internal workings of the mind and the external possibilities of random chance that take us by surprise— the things that happen to us in our lives and are totally out of our control.

Yet there is an answer, an internal place, which is heavier than the pressure of chaos, because it stays open in peaceful movement and trust. Trust in what...trust in the authenticity that is there within and is about to arise. Sometimes only in stilling the mind in contemplation can this authenticity be known and the truth of this very real moment right now. Sometimes we have to start dancing before we feel like dancing, and then the authentic spirit of dance suddenly overtakes us. So will the answer of what decision to make over take us, with the materialization of the authentic self, through allowing contemplation when we don't feel like it.

This materialization must take place in real time with the internal self, as the self meets the external world of choices. Only with the choice is the materialization complete. The materialization arrives during the moment of insight to cease acting like someone else. The moment of insight to act or cease acting based on the motivation of the fear of someone else. The decision to doubt my voice of despair that tells me there is no chance of change or good left in my life. The authentic self knows that I am valuable and would never doubt my ability to grow and change. I will honor this reality of my inherent worth.

I must always remind myself of three things, peace, hope and love, where are these three residing in me, and what influence do they have over me. Contemplation must lead me to these three things, for peace, hope and love are the creating force of authenticity within the self. The answer will always come when all three meet in harmonious resonance. The sound is unmistakable and unshakable. Possessing these three qualities does not allow us to forgo pain or suffering, they just give us the meaning to cope with them. Coping with skill of meaning making and creating meaning, is authenticity.

An answer will always be there, as the fog dissipates and the storm dies down, what is left standing is an authentic self, made of peace, hope and love. The answer does not have to be possessed by words, but can be contained in deeper knowing of intuitive gut instinct. Sometimes we have to live without words.

When there is stillness in the mind, contemplation can begin. When I am willing to push through with patience and trust, waiting for the eye of the storm, and embrace my subjective one of a kind self in harmony with my external conditions, and answer will come. Peace, Hope, and Love are speaking the answer in this very moment of our lives.

I know somewhere right now there is a highway waiting, there is a ship sailing and there is a plane above soaring to some destination unknown. I ask you, the unknown, where shall you take me, the destination is not my concern as much as my willingness to go, explore and be open to you. The unknown is calling, always, to some place deep inside of me; the *call* pulls me *inward* into subjective consciousness, and *outward* to that endless highway that is waiting. I must learn to practice going into the unknown, not as a conquistador, but as a humble and eager seeker made of clay and not stone, who is open to being reshaped.

There is a bed that rests underneath the stars, and there are no walls there to shelter me from nature, I am sleeping outside. My friends gather around me at night, and you talk, flirt and laugh until there is not a drop left to talk, flirt and laugh about. When I finally lay myself down to rest on this bed that lies under the stars, and in a town where the climate requires no blanket to keep warm, I find I do not want to sleep. No, I am too alive with the awe of waking consciousness, reverberating with the mystery of how I came to be in such a place as this. Before this night, I never knew that this possibility could exist. That life wants to make me feel this good.

I listen to a song called "Bad Dreams," by Damien Jurado, and I am filled with all these faint memories of all the bad things that have happened in my life—all the tragedies that befall us. I continue to stare up at the stars, not alone (my best friend is sleeping in a bed 5 feet to my left), and yet I am totally alone in my experience of this night and myself. Contemplation seems to synergize when we are able to find peace with our isolated subjective experiences of being totally alone.

All of the bad dreams I have lived in my life, in comparison to this moment, suddenly are swallowed up in the mystery and the unknown. I am lifted in heart 10 feet off my bed, and join the chorus of the stars singing above me, I am brought back down and bathe in the dirt of the ground below me, I am unified with this person to my left and the sacrifice of friendship given to me, I am layer upon layer given up to, and sifted by all knowing Peace, Hope and Love.

This moment only happened, because of a desire to go into the unknown, to a village and a country not my own. This night was a reward and an event, created from openness of heart to the hazards of exploring unknown territory. These things happen from a willingness to *approach and engage* life, rather than get swept away by indecision and ambivalence.

Ambivalence creates meaninglessness; decision creates unwavering commitment to purpose. The decision to be open and going into the unknown allows for openness to move towards life altering event. And yet I still somehow let this event and lesson go from my memory and personal practice.

What is the practice I must develop to continue to engage and encounter life? There needs to be a commitment to the mental practice of forgetting our assumptions, prejudice and fatalism. To approach the beginning of the day and week without believing I know what will or *has* to happen. I must arrive and show up at work with an attitude of openness. I must greet each new person without prejudice, for I might be greeting an angel. I have to learn to step into my day with the belief that all things are possible. The moment boredom and predictability leaks in, I begin this practice all over again, no matter how many times I fail or succeed.

I eventually fall asleep. This trip just kept getting better unraveling more eventful experiences. This trip eventually ended after two weeks. I basked in the afterglow for 6 months. Life conditions got better, and then they got really desperate, depressing and rat-race-delusional.

Then things went straight dreamy, and I held the prize of trusting and waiting to be able to go into the unknown again. The unknown started small, lasted for two weeks, then lasted for two years. I tried to live in the adventure, and then decided to venture on past the road, into truly unknown territory. The road ended into an abyss. I got lost inside myself and then I lost myself. I still return to these memories and present feelings that reside in me, and they call me onward into the unknown.

I know now that the condition of my heart needs to be beating towards openness, decision and resisting fatalism of all kinds. Contemplation allows me to hold this space and these moments that transcend time, by taking from the past and transmuting it into the present.

Contemplation keeps the sting of loss from overtaking me, and gives me a smile and hope. I am waiting for and in pursuit of life, not intimidated by the unknown. I am tamed by confidence, not shaken by present conditions, while all the while holding the value of what was. I will repeat and create a difference; I will not trust the mindlessness lie of despair, that nothing can be as good as what once was.

Trauma is a wound, a wound that lives off its own pain and defeat, and is always overtly and subtly aware of its injury. Trauma is an injury that keeps reinjuring itself. This hurting puts the owner of the wound in a repetitive loop of negative feedback, to be on repeat until the feedback is broken or released. Sometimes the feedback gets louder and louder building upon itself until the reverberation is so loud, that the fabric of reality is altered, and the world becomes a total dark, dire, barely habitable place of fear, distrust and hatred.

Sometimes the wound will take the place of total authority over the self, and is the only sure thing that feels real and is known. The painful memories become the one thing we trust. Perhaps this total power mimics the trauma society feels when inflicted by the force of absolute authority, found in totalitarianism.

Trauma sets itself up as the *dictator of despair*, canceling all known possibility of trustable good, of allowing vulnerability and love to be received and given in our life. Trauma is the impossible bad breaking in and questioning our desire to live life. Trauma pins us down, leaving us helpless to act, move or escape, and at its existential worst, causes us to fear the desire to want to love and trust in hope again.

Contemplation does not live in trauma, although contemplation is aware of the sting, the endless possibilities found in contemplation do not mix with traumas impact on removing possibility from our consciousness. Contemplation at its best breaks the negative feedback loop. I need to take my trauma into and be filtered by contemplation—allowing a new influence to break the feedback loop. I must stop trusting the negative thoughts and feelings of my traumas that bar me from entering contemplation.

This view of trauma through a contemplative lens is usually best done in the presence of a trustworthy other. When we can share our trauma with someone who is able to hold the good and bad of life in the same moment, we can begin to heal. There are parts of our lives that need to be witnessed by and shared with someone outside of ourselves. When we share these parts of our lives that have created states of helplessness and terror our psychological and emotional restoration beings. Through sharing our vulnerability and guilt, we see we are not as defected as we feel.

In psychology and mental health, there is the trauma-focused lens of viewing individuals. How a person's brain structure, physiology, social experience, and internal experience are all affected by traumatic experiences. There is hyper vigilance, rage, intense body reactions to perceptions of danger, no reaction to real danger and cognitive distortions (loud thoughts that break up and do not reflect the reality of the situation). There is a continually relived experience of helplessness in the traumatized individual, and that feeling affects those too who are trying to help those who have been traumatized. The weight of trauma needs to be verbalized and understood, before any attempt at taking contemplation seriously for help with trauma.

Contemplation in trauma is a step into the unknown, to allow another voice within to speak to all the negative feelings and memories. To allow the unconditional found in contemplation to rearrange trauma's message. In trauma the unconditional meaningless bad events: accidents, deaths, assaults, betrayals, bullying and abusive parents, form a message and experience that mimics the unconditional. There is a deposit left in us that seems to have a forever-negative balance.

Contemplation summons the call to see or seek the unconditional all around—to see all the bad running alongside parallel to the good, and to grab hold of both realities. In contemplation, perhaps just for 5 minutes we can jump totally into this river of good based in hope, peace and love. That is a call and a discipline to sing a dialectical song of unconditional good and unconditional bad, a song about trauma.

Beauty makes me want to weep,

Makes me want to swim way out into the sea and not come back

Makes me want to give it all away, then go hide from everyone I know

I don't want to sleep

I am so lovingly tonight, make me lovely tonight, while they are asleep

I can feel the beauty in the darkness

I can live in hope I can live in hope

Beauty makes me want to weep

Makes me want to keep every moment of my god-forsaken life in my mind

And not let go, and not let myself go and not let go,

I don't let fear go,

The power of the fear of being alive, I won't let it go,

When trauma is known and does not have the final blow

Is when I know I'm alive.

The reality and positive effects of chaos births possibility, and possibility is hope—hope is what sustains us in chaos, yet we still have an innate nature that rages against chaos. Possibility is hope because it instigates change, and without change, there would be no hope. Much of our time and brainpower is spent limiting our interactions with chaos, whether hiding our attention in entertainment and social media, or constantly planning and preparing for all the scenarios in our life. Anxiety is a smoke screen for the unpredictable chaotic fire that is the energy of the universe.

Anxiety is the somatic manifestation of chaos. Our anxiety increases or decreases with our ability to cope with our own internal chaos of loneliness and shame, and the external chaos of not being able to control our environment. We cannot forget to add into this chaos the mystery of the void, the eternal vastness of space, and the mysteries of existence. All of this leads us to either recognize or not accept the chaos—to acknowledge the possibility of hope and meaning within chaos.

Whether we look inward or outward, we will eventually find we are surrounded by all this randomness, and yet without chaos there would be no true possibility. When we come to see that chaos and hope are tied together, we can build resiliency (our ability to come back from defeat) and reframe our internal anxiety. When we do not run from the chaos...resist the chaos, we become something else.

The possibility that I am contemplating on is the kind that leads to unexpected impossible good—hope. The way I need to frame chaos is to see how chaos creates infinite possibility that eventually led to the existence of humanity. Science, theologians and philosophers cannot completely pinpoint how all this came to be, there is a bit of the *impossible* at work in the universe—and this *impossible* is because of the chaos. All the factors were here to create life, but how it emerged was chaotic, whether I trust the atheist or believer; there is more mystery to all of this than we usually like to admit. When we know that the chaos help create this impossibility of existence, we can have some assurance that the chaos in our internal and external world can produce some impossible good as well, can produce newness in despair.

The impossible good is the hope we need. Out of the chaos, we need to recognize that there is some new life or growth that is being formed and about to emerge— whether it is good or bad, is usually dependent on our willingness to embrace or reject change and transformation.

Soren Kierkegaard says that when we are in despair and have lost hope that we need to get possibility. I think through allowing ourselves to meditate on the reality of the chaotic universe, we find we know change will always occur. Therefore, in a very real objective sense *despair is not as real as feel it is,* except for the despair that resides in our minds and bodies. The inherit chaos in the universe prevents hopelessness and despair from having total reign.

Despair is really our minds tricking us to think that change is not possible, when the truth is that change is inevitable. When our minds are constantly ruminating and trying to make order out of chaos, there is a natural carry over into thinking that some things are permanent—it is a false yet very real sense of comfort. We need to make order in our minds, and we need to accept the reality of chaos and change. Developing a cognitive foundation of accepting Chaos.

I must also completely accept the chaos that suffering causes, and not put any limits on my ability to show empathy and action towards those in suffering—by allowing apathy to creep up in my acceptance. Acceptance cannot equal apathy.

Chaos creates tremendous amounts of suffering. We need to always be increasing our empathy and action towards helping those in suffering—and be challenging our minds to not give into despair in life. Victor Frankl gave us a beautiful framework in how to make meaning out of suffering, that even when we cannot change a situation due to death or victimization, we always have the freedom to change how we see and interpret that life event, I will quote him again, "to turn tragedy into triumph."

This leads us back to the beginning of how we cope and understand chaos. We ask ourselves constantly why something is happening to us, sometimes there is no why, there is only what is, and that what is chaos. Sometimes it is nobody's fault, not God's fault, your own or the governments; there is just the reality of chaos. Our mindset is what creates our realities of hope or despair.

I will in contemplation point my internal towards hope and possibility, with the foundation of knowing that chaos, can lead to good at any moment in life.

Working towards coming to peace and befriending the chaos in our lives is a worthy step towards spiritual growth. Reminding ourselves that we need to "get possibility" like Kierkegaard says, or know that chaos produces possibility and change, is salve to the anxious mind and gut. Remember that good can, and always will spontaneously emerge, just as we have emerged into a chaotic universe.

We have to survive in this world if we are going to survive. We make a choice to survive at some point in time, whether it is a conscious or biological choice, we decide. However, survival has no universal theme, for some survival means to have enough food at the end of the day and for others it means you have to survive systemic racism or other forms of marginalization. Nonetheless, survival is the core life force that drives us all the same.

What did I have to survive, what do I have to survive through now? I don't really want to acknowledge my struggle, doubt and fear, I would rather downplay my limitations than acknowledge my struggle for what it is, and was. Childhood isolation, the loss of a parent while fearing the loss of that same parent, disillusionment to the American dream and a mind that sought answers but constantly encountered the void. These things caused me great terror, sheer panic, wanting to run somewhere, but finding no escapes or places to find relief. It's like screaming run for your life, find shelter; the earth is about to explode!

For me to survive now I have to navigate through a society that has represented death to me, since I was 13 years old. I know now that the American dream is actual death for people of color, the environment, and the unconditional realities of beauty, and value outside of being a consumer. So how do I survive the death I feel all around me every day? I typically take a stoic malaise way of being, bite my upper lip and bite it as hard as I can, tell myself to shut up, get in my car, and make it through my day. That is how I survive; yet it has its costs. I have to pay for it with my vitality, my celebration of life and wonder in the impossible universe. A heavy price to pay for a game I don't even want to play.

I can be the rock of Gibraltar still—and I mean still as in future possibility and peace. I can be open and engaging with the unknown while living with responsibility and radical commitment to others. I can work towards what I believe in, the limitless value of the subjective experience of the individual and social justice.

When this call seems like it is not enough, is it that I am really saying that *I am not enough*? Am I not enough when I am sitting alone in an office or at home with nothing to do? That is what I have to face, that moment of nothingness, can that moment of nothingness be enough, and can I fill up that nothingness, void, and simply exist and be enough.

I have been trained in the art of boredom through a culture of immediate gratification, lust and shamed based marketing campaigns. When doing nothing, I am not good enough in the capitalist dream, or really the capitalist phantasmagoria. This ideology clearly has no use for me.

This ideology hates my dignity in simply being a human being. Oh, the disdain I see in society towards the homeless, as they sit and, "do nothing." In the American Dream they no longer become individuals anymore, just a scapegoat for our shame-based consumerism to be only doing. To be worth something while consuming nothing, that is my paradise lost, that is my great submission and commitment to love others and myself.

Where is despair leading me, but only to the place of despair, like gravity continually pulling me back to its heaviness again and again? I awake from dreams and despair is there to greet me first thing in the morning. Feeling trapped inside this temporal body, feeling chained to this rock, while the infinite universe is above me.

I do not dare to look at the reality of the moon, so close, or to the stars that represent all the possibilities that lie beyond our gravitational pull. For above the blue skies lies the, infinite-within-my-mental-grasp, and it causes me to hope or to despair. And so to if I look inward within my body I am confronted by the infinite universe of material atoms, which causes me to hope or despair—and if I despair to look inward or outward, I am led back to only heaviness, like a black hole of limitation, is the weight and pull of despair.

And yet why would a fragile animal have to confront such a silent invisible torment that leaves you without the ability to compare your situation with anyone else? When this despair feels like a stranger, but also like the one most known, whom can I trust? This despair is sleepy, and at points demands an answer. Right now despair just resides as an unwanted silent guest at the dining room table, with the gaze, will I engage? If I stay here, in this mental place, I could be lost forever in despair, this is what my mind fears most.

I am just a fragile animal with the weight of the universe in my chest, my mind gently demanding an answer for existence. When I turn to and welcome the unwanted guest's question, it rattles my bodily frame and my heart leaps. The fragile animal now knows Spirit, but will my spirit get hope and possibility, or transform me back into despair and limitation.

Kierkegaard says to know your weakness and then experience despair, is called a despair to will to not be oneself. I do not want to accept all of me; I'm ashamed of myself. When I despair, because of knowing my weakness of being the fragile animal, I run from the finite parts of myself.

This running is in an utter confused state, like a fugue, where one forgets their home, the faces of their children, and their name, as if it never existed. There is minimal meaning focusing only on the past, and only anxiety when focusing only on the future. This trauma of knowing my weakness seems too great to carry, and insanity seems the most honest and *real* thing to be. What is it to be real or to be a realized self, it is the realization of my weaknesses and limitations, and the infinite and limitless possibilities wrapped up in one body.

How can weakness know strength (the infinite)? Weakness does not want to know, because it is the antithesis of the infinite. Weakness can only become strength underneath the weight of suffering. When suffering is not lost to despair transforms us into the phoenix. So, in my greatest moments of weakness, if I let myself accept my limitations, accept all of me, then I will turn inward and see love and possibility, and now I am back in hope.

Suffering is the dialectical tension, when the weight of the infinite rests upon weakness and the individual is asked to rise up. When I am faced with my weakness and it speaks to me saying: the past has no meaning, the present is mundane and the future only has disappointments, this is a chance for transforming the touch of suffering, where I can run to despair (weakness) or to hope (possibilities).

If despair and weakness can be characterized by feelings of limitations, than to have hope can be characterized by accepting weakness, with humility, and the limitless infinite possibilities at every moment. Suffering will then fill us with a sense of openness and courage, when we stop resisting what we cannot change. When we stop resisting we then become something else, something new.

When death teaches me how to live, then I will truly know how to live. When I stop taking life for granted, I will know that I am living. Death is on my mind and rattles me to the marrow of my bones. Death is on my mind and that fear propels me to movement, purpose, and gratitude begins to fill up those same bones.

I fear the responsibility of what it means to be alive and be given the gift of me. Will I choke on the fear of failure, forcing me to choose apathy as my respirator and be the artificial life force that is barely keeping me alive? On the other hand, will I use the reality of death to bring me into living action and full engagement with everything today?

Our continual denial of thinking about and learning from the wisdom of death, for many, starts with religious beliefs. We verbalize and say this belief and we will be saved—death, punishment and the grave mean nothing to us, we only have to live half-heartedly in this world.

What an amazing relief to not fear death, I will just wait around for a bit, until I die, because this life does not matter, the next thing is the real thing. Death can be compartmentalized, put away and forgotten in the far recesses of our mind, and not used for a greater motivation to live now—a true deception.

I have heard it said that religion evolved into human culture, because the fear of death was so unbearable, that people came up with an afterlife to lessen the existential dread. This makes total and perfect sense, but this does not interest me anymore in my approach to death. I need a new approach to death, if I am to learn how to live now.

I must simply contemplate on death now and see what *comes up* inside of me, what it causes me to do. I need to allow that same survival instinct to avoid physical death to motivate and energize me spiritually, so that the same physical fear I would feel when the plane seems to be going down, I feel spiritually. The plane is going down spiritually when I am not fully engaged in my life. I am will be fully alive when I am consciously engaged in gratefulness in the here and now.

Death can motivate me to engage in life in *the here and now*. To be engaged, is to be simultaneously immersed in, and responding to the here of my *physical concrete surroundings*—and be fully accepting the *invaluable weight of this one and only instant* of *the present I inhabit*. This very moment, if we can slow down enough to be in it, is the only moment we can actually live. We are alive when we give ourselves the permission to be totally available outwardly and inwardly.

Contemplation is the paradox of total engagement with the non-subjective external reality, and internal subjective reality of the individual, the self. With our ability to contemplate death, we can hold and feel the value of our life. The clichés of bucket lists and if I died tomorrow hold wisdom. If I mock those things, it is evidence that I am living with a sense of false pride, and lacking the calm of humility. Here is my mantra into life.

If I was going to die next week...

Who would I hold tighter right now?

Whose smile would I want to hold onto forever?

What work would I put my hands and mind too with all my effort?

What view would I want to gaze out on?

What food should I savor just a little longer?

What song would I allow myself to recklessly dance without abandon?

What conversation would I melt into as time stopped?

What memory would I reflect on so I could savor the feeling of dissonant disappointments and triumphs?

What feeling would I conjure up inside myself to give off as a lasting fragrance to those who are around me?

Would I seek out a stranger to show unconditional acceptance in my kindness towards them?

Would I want to say goodbye or just hold onto these moments with you, without thinking about the end?

Would I continue to worry about the future and allow that to cloudy up my mind?

Would I walk instead of drive?

Would I cry instead of hide?

Would I contemplate for a little while and then give love,
peace and hope?

Would I ruminate on regrets, self-loathing and
comparisons instead of living right now?

Would I acknowledge my existence with a smile?

Close your eyes.

The end.

Made in the USA
Middletown, DE
04 December 2019